Written by:
Regina A. Bradley

Contributing Authors:
Elissa Yeates, Shashank Gokhale, Abby Hendricks

Edited by:
Emily Ramsower, Sandra J. Hoy

Cover Design:
Peter Licalzi

Printed in the United States of America

Table of Contents

INTRODUCTION

The PSAT is not only a great practice opportunity to get familiar with how the SAT is formatted, but also a chance to earn recognition as a National Merit Scholar. Since both the PSAT and the SAT are created by The College Board, the style of the exam is very similar, but is at a level better suited for what you have learned in school so far. There are a few differences which we will go over later, but it is important to know that much like the SAT, the biggest factor you will be tested on is:

How well you can take a test.

The big secret is that your knowledge alone won't get you the score you deserve; you have to learn specific skills for this exam.

The trick is not learning more, but perfecting what you have already learned, how it applies to the PSAT, and improving your test taking skills.

So, how do you prepare for the PSAT? What exactly does that mean "They are testing how well you can take a test"? Follow along with us and we will go through what the test is, what it means for you, and how you can prepare for it.

Here's what you have to go up against: First, the PSAT is a long test. Probably the longest test you've taken so far at a little bit over two hours long. Next, there are some tricks to watch out for that the test makers sneak in. Finally, there are techniques that you must implement not only for the actual test, but more importantly for studying to achieve your full potential. Your ability to handle these factors, as well as your skills in the tested materials, are needed to do well.

This book has everything you need to prepare for the PSAT, however it requires you to actively read it and utilize the information given and not just skim through it.Here's the good news though: you do not have to, and we do not want you, to sit for hours on end trying in vain to focus and study. This is counterproductive and will only waste your time, frustrate you, and result in a lower score than you deserve and are capable of making. By reading this guide, we will tell you how to most effectively use your time so you end up spending less time than you would otherwise. Good deal huh?

Our goal of this book is to cut through the nonsense and the clutter. We don't have a thousand pages of useless junk to make our book seem bigger or more important. We won't try to sell you on the idea that by doing a dozen practice tests, you will somehow get better. In reality, you would only be reinforcing the same mistakes you might already be making. This book is intended to be different, and it is different. It is written by tutors, from the perspective a tutor, because that's what you need now. You've obviously already had great teachers who do what they do best: teach you the subjects and the material. Teachers are not there to prepare you specifically for the PSAT, nor any other individual exam. So what you need now is that specialized person who knows the PSAT Reasoning exam backwards and forwards, and can show you how to apply that knowledge you have already learned to the best of your abilities for this exam.

Since this is likely your first introduction to the PSAT and SAT, it is important to understand what the PSAT is and is not. The PSAT is not used for college admissions unless you are one of the top scorers in the country. It serves two purposes: the first is to give you an opportunity to practice for the SAT, and the second is it is a test for the National Merit Scholarship Qualifying Test which only about the top 2% of test takers will achieve. So, even if you don't plan on making a run for the top 2% of scorers, this is still a great chance for you to improve! Below is a comparison chart of the PSAT and the SAT.

PSAT	**SAT**
A little over 2 hours Long	About 3.5 Hours Long
Not used for or seen by college admission	"Must have" for college admission
Three section scores between 20-80 (240 combined max score)	Three section scores between 200-800 (2400 combined max score)
No "high level" or "third year" math	Includes more difficult concepts and problems
Hardest math problems are typically last	Difficulty of math problems are mixed throughout
Two 25 minute critical reading sections	Three critical reading sections (70 minute total)
Two 25 minute math sections	Three math section (70 minute total)
One 30 minute "Writing Skills" section	Three writing sections (60 minute total)
"Writing Skills" has NO essay	1 written essay

Chapter 1: Let's Make a Plan

Although you won't use this test score for college admission, it is important to practice like it is the real thing. The first thing you need to do is develop a study plan. This will not only help you prepare for the PSAT, but will help you in the future when you take the SAT.Opening up practice questions and just jumping in won't help you at all. You need to find your strengths and weaknesses so you know where to focus your time. Doing practice tests will come later.

Your Plan for Studying

Schedule your study time :

To do well on the PSAT you need to schedule study time devoted to just this test. This will vary among students, depending on the number of test areas they feel they need more in depth review. Only you can determine that. However, even A students should schedule at least 2 uninterrupted hours a week for at least 8 weeks prior to the test. Scheduling this study time will have two important benefits: 1) you will feel more prepared which will reduce stress anxiety and 2) you will reduce the stress of trying to 'cram' before the test.

Schedule your breaks: break time is just as important and studying. If you have scheduled yourself for more than two consecutive hours of study, it is important to take a break, especially when changing study topic (ie math to reading). Getting up and moving not only gives the brain time to take in what you have already studied, but allows for increased circulation, sending oxygen to the brain faster which in turn makes it process better..

Write things down: this means use pen and paper. Yes, for those who haven't seen it, look to the left or right of your key board and you might find some. The act of physically transferring ink to paper will help you solidify what you are studying in your brain. Trust us on this, it will take more time while you study, but you won't waste time going back through over and over. This leads us into....

Actively Reading: Don't ever let yourself skim through subjects. You might as well turn your brain off and stare at the wall because you will get nothing out of your time. As you read, actively think about what you have read and what you will read. Writing down notes will help you with this! Your notes should be a summary of what you read, in your own words. Do not just copy the words you are reading down.

Practice Tests: Whatever you do, don't do half-hearted attempts at practice tests. You don't get smarter just because you wasted a few hours shuffling through some questions. When you are ready, sit down and do the test with a goal in mind. You might need to get familiar with the overall test and see the questions, so go through slowly the first time and don't worry about time. The next time, you might need to ID problem areas, This allow you to identify the topics you may need to spend more time on, so focus only on one section at a time. Later, you can do a full practice test for time. Just understand that you won't get better at the actual content just by having attempted a question, if anything it will reinforce mistakes you might be making. Eventually doing a full practice test is important however, because it will help you will train your brain to switch gears when needed and work on the ability to stay focused for the marathon on test day.

Sleep: no surprise here, you need sleep. To prepare yourself and help beat your own nerves when test day comes, get in the habit now of following the same routine each night and going to bed at the same time. Lying awake staring at the ceiling the entire night before the test won't do much good for your score.

Short Term Goals: Set yourself some goals for each day or week. This will help you stay focused on a subject or topic so you don't lose track. There is a lot to study, and you need to be sure you are going through systematically so you don't waste time jumping around from section to section.

Study locations: Library: good. In front of TV: bad. Find a quiet relaxing place that you can dedicate as a "study zone". This should NOT be your bed, or the couch, or anywhere else you use for sleeping, eating, or relaxing. If you sit at your desk at home or in the library, you won't be tempted to "just watch tv for just a few minutes" or start getting sleeping and nod off because you are in bed already.

Finally, and most importantly: Set yourself a specific goal for your test score and work towards that. Be sure it's a realistic goal though. This way, when you take practice tests and see your scores, you will know what you need to focus on and work towards. If you don't do this, you can easily end up being content with whatever your score happens to be, meaning you could be missing valuable and easily attainable points. We'll cover this more later, but you need to look at universities requirements, your grades, and other things to determine what that score needs to be. Doing the full practice test can give you a good idea of what range your score will be in.

Your Plan for Test Day

Cramming: don't do this. Please. It will only stress you out more if you are already feeling anxious. And really...come on...do you think you'll actually accomplish something in a couple hours that you couldn't in the weeks you spent studying beforehand??

Food: Eat a good healthy dinner the night before, with some good carbohydrates. You are really getting ready for a marathon whether you know it or not, just that your brain is going to be doing the work. The day of, avoid excess coffee or caffeine and have a good breakfast that won't bog you down. Fruits, grains, etc will boost your energy and keep you full. Sugar is to your brain what oxygen is to your lungs, and good healthy foods will provide a steady supply of that sugar. Do not, do not, do not try to substitute sugary candies or sodas because it won't work the same way! You'll get a big bolus of sugar and then your energy and your test score will crash through the floor.

Think positively: Seriously! It may sound silly, but if you are thinking of gloom and doom you will have a self-fulfilling prophecy of a lower score than you should get. Literally imagine yourseseeing questions and thinking confidently "Hey, I know this answer! I studied for this topic!".

Be bold: Don't second guess questions. You need to be bold and go with your gut instinct, but don't be careless either. Make your decision and move forward. Worrying about a question you answered two pages ago while working a current problemwon't help you at that moment, you can always use any remaining time when you've reached the end of the test to go back over questions

Don't Panic: Don't rush and don't worry about the clock or what everyone else is doing. Even if you knew you had 5 minutes left or that everyone else was further along then you, how on earth is that going to help you on YOUR test? If you have followed this guide you will know your own pace which is all that matters.

Tough questions: Don't waste your time on the questions you find to be overly difficult on test day. The test makers will purposefully throw in a few overly complicated problems to throw you off your game. Get the points you can while you can and come back later if you have time. We'll go over the specifics of this strategy later in the individual sections.

Gum: About 10 cents can not only buy you a stick of gun, but it can also buy you twenty or more focused minutes. No joke. Studies have actually found that students who chew gum during a test do in fact score higher on average than those who don't. Why? It keeps you awake and your brain working so you in turn stay focused on the task at hand. Find your favorite flavor and don't leave home without it on test day. Just double check beforehand as to whether or not your testing center allows gum.

<u>What to Bring:</u> You MUST have your admission ticket, two No. 2 pencils and a soft eraser, your photo ID, and an acceptable calculator (graphing or scientific is best; not 4 function). You SHOULD bring a watch you are familiar with and have used during your practice test, extra batteries for your calculator, a bag or backpack for your belongings so you aren't juggling everything, and drinks and snacks for breaks.

<u>What to leave at home:</u> don't bring scratch paper, notes or books, cell phones, MP3 players/iPods, highlighters and colored pencils, a timer (like a kitchen timer), or any type of photographic equipment or listening/recording device.

Chapter 2: Study Tricks, Tips, and Cautions

You need to become intimately aware of how the PSAT is formatted. As we mentioned earlier, this exam does not really test your specific knowledge as much as it does your ability to think and reason. Instead, it uses your knowledge as a way to test your ability to reason. For example, a question might only require basic math, but they will throw in extra information as distracter. If you aren't ready for it, you'll waste time or worse yet, get a wrong answer because you were too focused on the extra stuff.

Everyone has both strengths and weaknesses and you need to identify yours. Be honest, maybe you just aren't as good at math as you would like to be. This is your opportunity to improve. Don't forget to use your strengths, but if you are only getting 75% of the math portion right, and 95% of the verbal correct, you have a lot more points you could be making on math. So, do not waste your efforts making yourself feel better by only continuing to ace the verbal...start working on getting better at math and pick up those extra points!

Only answer what is asked. Don't try to be clever or read between the lines. One thing The College Board never does is write questions so you need extraneous knowledge to answer a questionIf you see something just seems really complicated or out of place, or requires lengthy calculations, odds are they put it there just for that reason. Luckily for you, you are reading this right now, so you you know to avoid unnecessary calculations. Just answer what is asked, and that's it!

Next, don't assume there is a specific order to the answer choices. For example, you have answered "C" fifteen times in a row. That must be wrong? Is this a trick? Did you mess something up? The answer is simple: No. It's not a trick, and you didn't do anything wrong. It's going to happen to you, so don't worry or even think about it when it does. The corresponding letters to the questions are weighted so that there is an equal number of each, however, their order is computer generated. Regardless, it doesn't matter just mark your answers and don't let it distract you!

Just like the SAT, on the PSAT, you do not lose points for unanswered questions, but you lose a fraction of a point for wrong answers. So, you've got to weigh your options here. What we have found works best is narrowing your options down to two choices, then you have a 50% chance of making a point and a 50% chance of only losing a fraction of a point. Statistically, you will have more points won that you would lose. Go with your gut on the answer you think is right. If you just really aren't sure, move on and come back later. Guess what else? There are questions that want "the best answer".... so there could be a reason why both answers seem correct: because they are! You don't want to leave points on the table, but you need to exercise caution so you don't give them away a fraction at a time either.

Finally, the best way to accomplish all this is to develop a system for marking off the answers you know are wrong. Never mark on the answer sheet though, because you don't want any stray marks getting left behind. Stay consistent withyour marking system so you don't have to think "wait, did that circle mean it's good or did that check mark mean it's good? What about that "x"?"

An important aspect to consider is when to really dig in and start studying. An easy way to do it is to base it on when you will be taking the test, rather than studying and then seeing what test dates are available. Visit collegeboard.org and see what dates are available and find a location in your area, preferably one you are familiar with. Work backwards to figure out how many weeks or months you have prior to the test and make yourself a schedule, being sure to leave an extra few weeks just in case you need a little more time.

Chapter 3: The Math Section

The PSAT Math Section will test your knowledge of the following concepts:

- numbers and operations
- algebra
- geometry
- data analysis
- statistics
- probability

Before you take the PSAT, you need to have a good understanding of the math topics covered and sharpen your basic skills. This section will explain what math areas are covered on the exam with detailed examples. However, this section is NOT designed to TEACH you math. The standard math test on the PSAT covers math concepts learned through Algebra I, so you shouldn't need to learn any new skills.

About the Math Section
You will be answering two types of questions:
- Problem solving (multiple choices)
- Student response questions (also known as grid-ins)

Math questions on the PSAT follow an order of difficulty; the questions start out easy, move to medium-level difficulty, and end with the most difficult questions. But remember that these terms are dependent on the individual. You might find manipulating polynomials easy and geometry difficult, whereas it may be the opposite for the person sitting next to you. So, DO NOT ANSWER THE QUESTIONS IN ORDER! Instead, read the questions and if how to solve it comes to mind right away, do so and move on. If you aren't sure about what concept is being tested or how to solve that question, skip it and move on. Answer the questions in *your* order of difficulty, saving the most difficult for last. If a question begins to take too long, you may have to give it up and continue. When you encounter a difficult problem, you have two choices:

1) Stop. Move on. Come back if you have time.
2) Eliminate at least one of the answer choices. Make your best guess. Move on.

Grid-In/Student Provided Responses
The student-produced response questions require you to supply the correct answer. Answer choices are not given; instead, you fill in the grid with your response. You won't be able to make an educated guess and eliminate choices. However, there is *no wrong-answer penalty* on grid-ins. Always put something down, even if you are not certain it is the correct answer.

Important things to know about grid-ins:

- There are no negative answers. If you get a negative answer, you made a mistake.
- There can be more than one correct answer. If you find two or more answers, pick one and move on.
- There are no mixed numbers. Convert all improper fractions to simple fractions or decimals.
- Do not put a zero before a decimal point. Instead of gridding in 0.22, grid in .22. With decimals, particularly repeating decimals, do not round up. Start with the bubble on the far left and fill in all four spaces. You won't be penalized for not rounding up but you will be penalized if you round up improperly.

Math Areas of the PSAT

You have a much better chance of getting a good PSAT math score if you know what to expect. Focusing your study time on what will be included in the math sections of the PSAT and not wasting your time with areas that won't be included can help you achieve a higher score. The PSAT covers math up to, and including, the first semester of Algebra II.

Here's how the creators of the PSAT describe the breakdown of the test:

- Numbers and operation
- Algebra and functions (though not content covered in third-year math classes—content that will appear on the PSAT)
- Geometry and measurement
- Data analysis, statistics, and probability

Math skills that you will not need for the PSAT:

- Working with bulky numbers or endless calculations
- Writing geometry proofs
- Working with imaginary numbers or the square roots of negative numbers
- Trigonometry or calculus

Calculators

Even though you are allowed to use a calculator, don't rely on it. Actually, the less you use it, the better. If it were possible to answer every question on the PSAT by simply plugging numbers into your calculator, you wouldn't be allowed to have one. If you see a question requiring heavy calculations, you are most likely missing the point of the question. Remember the creators of the exam designed this to be a timed test that any attentive high school student could score well on without a calculator. Typically, your calculator will come in handy to do basic math and to check your work. You'll have to use your brain for the reasoning!

The Most Common Mistakes

Here is a list of the six most common mistakes test takers make on the PSAT, starting with the most common.

- Answer with the wrong sign (positive / negative)
- Working questions in order
- Order of Operation errors when solving
- Misplaced decimal
- Solution does not respond to what was asked for in the question
- Circling the wrong letter or filling in wrong circle

If you are thinking, "Those ideas are just common sense"--exactly! Most of the mistakes made on the PSAT are simple mistakes. Regardless, they still result in a wrong answer and penalty.

Strategies

Do not treat your study time for the PSAT as if it were a normal homework assignment. You must utilize the following strategies while you study for the PSAT:

1) Go back to the basics – practice your basic skills such as sign changes, order of operations, simplifying fractions and equation manipulation. These are the skills you will use the most on PSAT, but they will be applied in different contexts. Remember, when it comes right down to it, there are only four basics used to solve any math problem: adding, subtracting, multiplying and dividing. The only thing that changes is the order in which they are used to solve the problem.

2) Don't rely on mental math – using mental math is great for eliminating answer choices, but ALWAYS WRITE IT DOWN! This cannot be stressed enough. Use your paper and booklet; by writing and/or drawing out the problem, you are more likely to catch common mistakes. Just the act of writing something down for every question leads to an improvement in your PSAT score by forcing you to organize your calculations. Use your calculator to *check* your work.

3) The three times rule –

1) **Read the question**, write the given information.
2) **Read the question**, set up equation(s), and solve.
3) **Read the question**, make sure your answer makes sense (is the amount too large or small, is the answer in the correct unit of measure, etc.).

4) Making an educated guess – eliminate at least one answer choice as most probably incorrect and guess the most likely correct from the remaining choices. Educated guessing is critical to increasing your score. Often, there will be at least one answer choice that is obviously incorrect--provided you look for it.

5) Pacing yourself – although this is a timed test, accuracy is more important than speed. Remember to go through a section and answer all the questions that are easy for you. Determine the amount of time you have left to spend on each problem. Go through a second time to solve the remaining questions; if you are taking longer than your calculated time, make an educated guess and move on.

6) Avoid easy answers – the correct answer is seldom the one that looks correct at first glance, even for easy questions (this is where the 'common sense' mistakes occur). ALWAYS check your answers, even for the 'easy' questions. Answers that seem to jump out are called PSAT distracters and are designed to catch the eye of students rushing through the test. More often than not, an answer choice for a hard item that looks too good to be true probably is.

PSAT Formulas and Facts (Given)

The following formulas will be provided on the exam; however, there will be no descriptions or example of how to use them.

- Radius and Circumference of a Circle

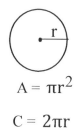

$$A = \pi r^2$$

$$C = 2\pi r$$

- Area of a rectangle

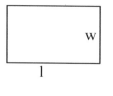

$$A = lw$$

- Area of a Triangle

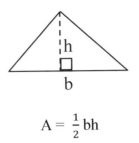

$$A = \frac{1}{2}bh$$

- Volume of a Cube

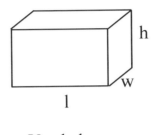

$$V = lwh$$

- Volume of a Cylinder

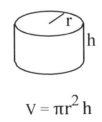

$$V = \pi r^2 h$$

- The Pythagorean Theorem – How to Find a Diagonal Length

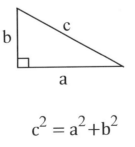

$$c^2 = a^2 + b^2$$

- Special Right Triangles

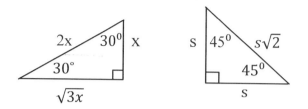

- The number of degrees of an arc in a circle is 360.
- The measure of degrees of a straight angle is 180.
- The sum of degrees of the angles in a triangle is 180.

Make sure you are familiar with using the above formulas – including manipulating them as needed for questions you will encounter on the test since they will not always be straightforward. For example:

$$\text{If} \quad A = 1/2bh \quad \text{then} \quad h = (2A)/b$$

PSAT Formulas, Facts and Terms (Not Given)

The next few pages will cover various math subjects (starting with the basics, but in no particular order) along with worked examples. If you are taking the PSAT, you have already had course instruction in these areas. Keep in mind that this is a guide to what you can expect to encounter on the Math PSAT and is not a comprehensive lesson to teach you everything you have been taught previously in school.

You need to practice in order to score well on the test. To make the most out of your practice, use this guide to determine the areas in which you need more review and practice all areas under test circumstances. Do not time yourself on the first practice test. You should take your time and let your brain recall the math necessary to solve the questions, using the examples given to 'jog' your memory. Then, when you feel you are ready, begin taking timed tests. This is another important part of scoring well on the PSAT: knowing your strong areas and the average amount of time it takes to solve the problems. This knowledge also helps relieve stress while taking the test. Practice exams can help you become familiar with the types of questions, how many there are, and what to expect.

TEST SECRET
DO NOT go through countless practice exams as a means to become "better" at math. Going through all those exams will take too much time, burn you out, and it won't help!

If you find yourself needing additional help with math concepts after reviewing the following information, refer to the "Math Resources" chapter at the end of this book.

- Order of Operations

  PEMDAS – **P**arentheses/**E**xponents/**M**ultiply/**D**ivide/**A**dd/**S**ubtract

- Positive & Negative Number Rules

  (+) + (-) = subtract the two numbers, solution gets the sign of the larger number

  (-) + (-) = negative number

  (-) x (-) = positive number

  (-) / (-) = positive number

  (-) / (+) = negative number

  (-) x (+) = negative number

- Absolute Value

  The absolute value of a number is its distance from zero, not its value.

  Example:
  $|3| = 3$ and $|-3| = 3$

- Arithmetic Sequence

  Each term is equal to the previous term plus x.

  Example: 2, 5, 8, 11 $x = 3$
  3+2 = 5, 3+5 = 8, 3+8 = 11…

- Geometric Sequence
  Each term is equal to the previous term multiplied by x.

  Example: 2, 4, 8, 16 $x = 2$
  2x2 = 4, 2x4 = 8, 2x8 = 16…

- Prime Factorization
  Expand to prime number factors.
  Example: 104 = 2 x 2 x 2 x 13

  Multiply common prime factors

  Example: 28 = 2 x 2 x 7
              80 = 2 x 2 x 2 x 5

- Greatest Common Factor (GCF)

  The greatest factor that divides two numbers.

  Example: the GCF of 24 and 18 is 6. 6 is the largest number, or greatest factor, that can divide both 24 and 18.

- Percent, Part, & Whole

  part = percent x whole

  percent = part / whole

  whole = part / percent

  Example: Jim spent 30% of his paycheck at the fair. He spent $15 for a hat, $30 for a shirt, and spent $20 playing games. How much was his check? (round to nearest dollar)

  ANSWER: whole = 65 / .30 = $217.00

TEST SECRET

Remember, you must put the % into decimal form before solving!

  For more help on Percent, Part, & Whole, see Section 1 of the Math Question Bank.

- Percent Change
  - Percent change = amount of change / original amount x 100
  - Percent increase = (new amount   original amount) / original amount x 100
  - Percent decrease = (original amount – new amount) / original amount x 100
  - Amount increase (decrease) = original price x percent markup (markdown)
  - Original price = new price / (whole - percent markdown)
  - Original price = new price / (whole + percent markup)

  Example: A car that was originally priced at $8300 has been reduced to $6995. What percent has it been reduced?

  (8300 – 6995) / 8300 x 100 = 15.72%

  ANSWER: 15.72%

  For more help on Percent Change, see Section 1 of the Math Question Bank.

- Repeated Percent Change

  Increase: Final amount = original amount x $(1 + rate)^{\text{\# of changes}}$

  Decrease: Final Amount = original amount x $(1 - rate)^{\text{\#of changes}}$

Example: The weight of a tube of toothpaste decreases by 3% each time it is used. If it weighed 76.5 grams new, what is its weight in grams after 15 uses?

Final amount = 76.5 x $(1 - .3)^{15}$

ANSWER = 76.5 x $(.97)^{15}$ = 48.44 grams

TEST SECRET

This formula is used to calculate annual bank interest problems with number of years being the exponent.

For more help on Repeated Percent Change, see Section 1 of the Math Question Bank.

- Simple Interest

    Interest x Principle

    Example: If I deposit $500 in an account with an annual rate of 5%, how much will I have after 2 years?

    1st yr   500 + (500 x .05) = 525
    2nd yr   525 + (525 x .05) = 551.25
    ANSWER: $551.25

    For more help on Simple Interest, see Section 1 of the Math Question Bank.

- Ratios

    To solve a ratio simply find the equivalent fraction. To distribute a whole across a ratio:

    1. Total all parts.
    2. Divide the whole by the total number of parts.
    3. Multiply quotient by corresponding part of ratio.

    Example: There are 90 voters in a room, who are either Democrat or Republican. The ratio of Democrats to Republicans is 5:4, how many Republicans are there?

    Step 1   5 + 4 = 9
    Step 2   90 / 9 = 10
    Step 3   10 x 4 = 40
    ANSWER: 40 Republicans

    For more help on Ratios, see Section 10 of the Math Question Bank.

- Proportions

    Direct Proportions: corresponding ratio parts change in the same direction (increase/decrease).

    Indirect Proportions: corresponding ratio parts change in opposite directions; as one part increases the other decreases.

    Example: A train traveling 120 miles takes 3 hours to get to its destination. How long will it take if the train travels 180 miles?
    120mph: 180mph   is to x hours:3 hours (write as fraction and cross multiply)
    $120/3 = 180/x$
    $540 = 120x$
    $x = 4.5$ hours

    For more help on Proportions, see Section 10 of the Math Question Bank.

- Mean

    Mean is a math term for "average." Total all terms / number of terms.

    Example: What is the average of 2, 10, 17, and 30?
    $(2+10+17+30)/4 = 14.75$
    ANSWER: 14.75

    The following is an example of a mean problem with missing information.

    Example: Cory averaged 3 hits per game over the course of 5 baseball games. He had 2 hits in the first and fourth games, 3 hits in the second game, and 4 hits in his last game. How many hits did he have in his second game?
    Step 1:   Determine total. 3 hits x 5 games = 15 hits
    Step 2:   Determine known total. $2 + 2 + 3 + 4 = 11$
    Step 3:   Subtract. $15 - 11 = 4$
    ANSWER: 4 hits in his second game

- Median

    The median is the middle number of a given set. In the case of a set of even numbers, the middle two numbers are averaged (mean).

    Example: What is the average of 1, 2, 3, 4, 5, 6, & 7?
    ANSWER: 4

Example: What is the median of 1, 2, 3, 4, 5, 6, 7, & 8?
ANSWER: 4.5

- Mode

The mode is the number that occurs most frequently within a given set.

Example: what is the mode of 1, 2, 4, 3, 2, 5, 6, 7, 7, 2?
ANSWER: 2

For more help on Mean/Median/Mode, see Section 2 of the Math Question Bank.

- Combined Average

Working a combined average problem is similar to finding a simple average, except you must weight each average before determining the sum.

Example: If Cory averaged 3 hits per game during the summer and 2 hits per game during the fall and played 7 games in the summer and 8 games in the fall, what was his hit average overall?

Step 1: Weight each average. Summer: $3 \times 7 = 21$
Fall: $2 \times 8 = 16$
Sum $= 37$

Step 2: Total number of games. $7 + 8 = 15$
Step 3: Calculate average. $37/15 = {\sim}2.47$ hits/game

ANSWER: Approximately 2.47 hits per game

How to work a combined average problem with a missing term:
Example: Bobbie paid an average of $20 a piece for ten shirts. If five of the shirts averaged $15 each, what was the average cost of the remaining shirts?

Step 1: Calculate sum $10 \times 20 = 200$
Step 2: Calculate sub-sum #1 $5 \times 15 = 75$
Step 3: Calculate sub-sum #2 $200 - 75 = 125$
Step 4: Calculate average $125 / 5 = 25$

ANSWER: $25

For more help on Combined Averages, see Section 2 of the Math Question Bank.

- Exponent Rules
  - $x^0 = 1$ Example: $5^0 = 1$
  - $x^1 = x$ Example: $5^1 = 5$
  - $x^a \cdot x^b = x^{a+b}$ Example: $5^2 \times 5^3 = 5^5$
  - $(xy)^a = x^a y^a$ Example: $(5 \times 6)^2 = 5^2 \times 6^2 = 25 \times 36$
  - $(x^a)^b = x^{ab}$ Example: $(5^2)^3 = 5^6$
  - $(x/y)^a = x^a/y^a$ Example: $(10/5)^2 = 10^2/5^2 = 100/25$
  - $x^a/y^b = x^{a-b}$ Example: $5^4/5^3 = 5^1 = 5$ (remember $x \neq 0$)
  - $x^{1/a} = \sqrt[a]{x}$ Example: $25^{1/2} = \sqrt[2]{25} = 5$
  - $x^{-a} = \dfrac{1}{x^a}$ Example: $5^{-2} = \dfrac{1}{5^2} = \dfrac{1}{25}$ (remember $x \neq 0$)
  - $(-x)^a$ = positive number if a is even; negative number if a is odd

TEST SECRET

It is crucial that you know how to simplify and solve exponents and roots on the PSAT. Practice these as much as needed until you master them!

Example: Simplify the following: $\dfrac{(3^{-1}a^4 b^{-3})^{-2}}{(6a^2ab^{-1}c^{-2})^2}$

$$\frac{(3^{-1}a^4 b^{-3})^{-2}}{(6a^2ab^{-1}c^{-2})} = \frac{3^2 a^{-8} b^6}{6^2 a^4 b^{-2} c^{-4}}$$

$$= \frac{9a^{-8}b^6}{36a^4b^{-2}c^{-4}} = \frac{b^6 b^2 c^4}{4a^4 a^8} = \frac{b^8 c^4}{4a^{12}}$$

ANSWER: $= \dfrac{b^8 c^4}{4a^{12}}$

To add or subtract equations with exponential terms, calculate the term value then add/subtract.

Example: $18^0 - 3 + 2^4 = 1 - 3 + 16 = 14$

     ANSWER: 14

For more help on Exponents, see Section 3 of the Math Question Bank.

- Roots

Root of a Product: $\sqrt[n]{a \cdot b} = \sqrt[n]{a} \cdot \sqrt[n]{b}$

Root of a Quotient: $\sqrt[n]{\dfrac{a}{b}} = \dfrac{\sqrt[n]{a}}{\sqrt[n]{b}}$

Fractional Exponent: $\sqrt[n]{a^m} = a^{m/n}$

Example: Simplify the following:

$$\frac{2(6 - 3\sqrt{5})}{(6 + 3\sqrt{5})(6 - 3\sqrt{5})}$$

$$= \frac{12 - 6\sqrt{5}}{6^2 - (3\sqrt{5})^2}$$

$$= \frac{12 - 6\sqrt{5}}{6^2 - (3\sqrt{5})^2} = \frac{12 - 6\sqrt{5}}{6^2 - (3 \times 3 \times \sqrt{5} \times \sqrt{5})}$$

$$= \frac{12 - 6\sqrt{5}}{6^2 - (9 \times 5)} = \frac{12 - 6\sqrt{5}}{36 - 45} = \frac{12 - 6\sqrt{5}}{-9} = -\frac{(12 - 6\sqrt{5})}{9}$$

$$= -\frac{3(4 - 2\sqrt{5})}{9} = -\frac{(4 - 2\sqrt{5})}{3} = \frac{-4 + 2\sqrt{5}}{3}$$

$$= \frac{-4 + 2\sqrt{5}}{3}$$

ANSWER: $= \dfrac{-4 + 2\sqrt{5}}{3}$

For more help on Roots, see Section 3 of the Math Question Bank.

- Algebraic Equations

    When simplifying or solving algebraic equations, you need to be able to utilize all math rules: exponents, roots, negatives, order of operations, etc.

    1. Add & Subtract: only the coefficients of like terms.
        Example:
        $$5xy + 7y + 2yz + 11xy - 5yz = 16xy + 7y - 3yz$$

    2. Multiplication: first the coefficients, then the variables.
        Example: monomial x monomial
        $$(3x^4y^2z)(2y^4z^5) = 6x^4y^6z^6$$
        (a variable with no exponent has exponent of 1)

        Example: monomial x polynomial
        $$(2y^2)(y^3 + 2xy^2z + 4z) = 2y^5 + 4xy^4z + 8y^2z$$

        Example: binomial x binomial
            (remember **FOIL** – **F**irst, **O**uter, **I**nner, **L**ast)

        $$(5x + 2)(3x + 3)$$

First	$5x \cdot 3x = 15x^2$	
Outer	$5x \cdot 3 = 15x$	
Inner	$2 \cdot 3x = 6x$	
Last	$2 \cdot 3 = 6$	

        Combine like terms. $15x^2 + 21x + 6$

        Example: binomial x polynomial
        $$(x + 3)(2x^2 - 5x - 2)$$
        First term $x(2x^2 - 5x - 2) = 2x^3 - 5x^2 - 2x$
        Second term $3(2x^2 - 5x - 2) = 6x^2 - 15x - 6$
        Add $2x^3 + x^2 - 17x - 6$

    3. Division: same as multiplying. Be sure to follow exponent and root rules!

    4. Difference of squares: remember **FOIL** – **F**irst, **O**uter, **I**nner, **L**ast
        Examples:
        $$a^2 - b^2 = (a + b)(a - b)$$
        $$a^2 + 2ab + b^2 = (a + b)(a + b)$$
        $$a^2 - 2ab + b^2 = (a - b)(a - b)$$

30

TEST SECRET

It is crucial that you know how to simplify and solve algebraic equations containing multiple exponents, variables and roots. The PSAT will have problems that contain multiple equations all in one problem, so practice these specific skills!

For more help on Algebraic Equations, see Section 4 of the Math Question Bank.

- Inequalities

    Inequalities are solved like linear and algebraic equations, except the sign must be reversed when working with a negative.

    Example: Solve: $-7x + 2 < 6 - 5x$
    Step 1: Combine like terms. $-2x < 4$
    Step 2: Solve for x. Reverse sign. $x > -2$
           ANSWER: $x > -2$

    Solving compound inequalities will give you two answers.

    Example: Solve: $-4 \le 2x - 2 \le 6$
    Step 1: Add 2 to each term to isolate x.
    $-2 \le 2x \le 8$
    Step 2: Divide by 2.
    $-1 \le x \le 4$
           ANSWER: Solution set is [-1, 4]

    For more help on Inequalities, see Section 5 of the Math Question Bank.

- Literal Equations

    These are equations with more than one variable. Solve in terms of one variable first.

    Example: Solve for y: $6x = 9y = 1/3y + 3x$
    Step 1: Combine like terms. $9y - 1/3y = 3x - 6x$
                                 $26/3y = -3x$
    Step 2: Solve for y. $y = -9x/26$
           ANSWER: $y = -9x/26$

    For more help on Literal Equations, see Section 5 of the Math Question Bank.

- Linear Systems

    A linear system requires the solving of two literal equations simultaneously. There are two different methods (Substitution and Addition) that can be used to solve linear systems on the PSAT.

    <u>Substitution Method</u>: Solve for one variable in one equation and substitute it into the other equation.
    Example: Solve $3y - 4 + x = 0$ and $5x + 6y = 11$

        Step 1: Solve for one variable.
            $$3y - 4 + x = 0$$
            $$3y + x = 4$$
            $$x = 4 - 3y$$

        Step 2: Substitute into second equation, and solve.
            $$5(4 - 3y) + 6y = 11$$
            $$20 - 15y + 6y = 11$$
            $$20 - 9y = 11$$
            $$-9y = -9$$
            $$y = 1$$

        Step 3: Substitute into first equation.
            $$3(1) - 4 + x = 0$$
            $$-1 + x = 0$$
            $$x = 1$$

        ANSWER: solution is $x = 1$, $y = 1$

    <u>Addition Method</u>: Manipulate one of the equations so that when added to the other, one variable is eliminated.

    Example: Solve $2x + 4y = 8$ and $4x + 2y = 10$

        Step 1: Manipulate one equation to eliminate a variable when added together.

            $$-2(2x + 4y = 8) =$$
            $$-4x - 8y = -16$$
            $$+ 4x + 2y = 10$$
            $$-6y = -6 \quad y = 1$$

        Step 2: Plug into an equation and solve for the other variable.

$$2x + 4(1) = 8$$
$$2x + 4 = 8$$
$$2x = 4 \qquad x = 2$$

ANSWER: solution is $x = 2$, $y = 1$

Example: The following is a typical PSAT word problem that would use a linear system to solve.

Tommy has a collection of coins worth $5.20. He has 8 more nickels than quarters. How many of each does he have?

Step1: Set up equations. Let n = nickels and q = quarters. Drop the 0.	$.05n + .25q = 5.2$ $n = q + 8$
Step 2: Substitute equation 2 into equation 1.	$.05(q+8) + .25q = 5.2$
Step 3: Solve for q. You can ignore the decimal point and negative sign after this step because you are solving for number of coins.	$-.05(q+8) + .25q = 5.2$ $.05q+.4+.25q = 5.2$ $q = 16$
Step 4: Plug into other equation.	$n = q + 8 \qquad n = 24$

Solution: 16 quarters, 24 nickels

Step 5: Check your answer.	$24(.05) + 16(.25) = \$5.20$ $\$1.20 + \$4.00 = \$5.20$

ANSWER: 16 quarters, 24 nickels

For more help on Linear Systems, see Section 5 of the Math Question Bank.

- Rate of Change

    Used to describe the change in one variable with respect to another. The average rate of change of y with respect to x is: change in y / change in x.

    Example: The percentage of the U.S. population living in rural areas decreased from 84.7% in 1850 to 21.0% in 2000. What was the average rate of change in the rural population annually over that time period?

Step 1: Set up the equation putting the dependent variable in the numerator.

change in % /change in years
(21.0 – 84.7)/ (2000-1850) =
-63.7% / 150 years
~ - 0.42 years

Since the problem stated a decrease, a negative answer is correct. The population decreased on average .42% each year.

ANSWER: .42% each year

For more help on Rate of Change, see Section 10 of the Math Question Bank.

- Slope (m)

  The same formula is used to calculate the slope (m) of a straight line connecting two points.
  $m = (y_2 – y_1) / (x_2 – x_1)$ = change in y / change in x

  Example: Calculate slope of the line in the diagram.

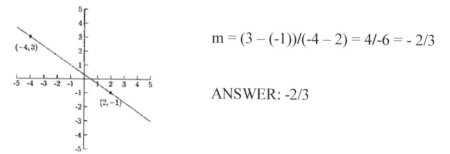

$$m = (3 – (-1))/(-4 – 2) = 4/-6 = - 2/3$$

ANSWER: -2/3

For more help on Slope, see Section 6 of the Math Question Bank.

- Distance and Midpoint

  To determine the distance between two points from a grid use the formula:

  $$d = \sqrt{(x_2 - x_1)^2 + (y_2 - y_1)^2}$$

  Example: What is the distance between point (3, -6) and (-5, 2)?

  $$d = \sqrt{(-5 - 3)^2 + (2 - (-6))^2} \;=\; \sqrt{64 + 64} = \sqrt{64 \times 2} \;=\; 8\sqrt{2}$$

  To determine the midpoint between two points:
    - add the two x coordinates together and divide by 2 (midpoint x)
    - add the y coordinates together & divide by 2 (midpoint y)

  $$= \left(\frac{x_1 + x_2}{2} , \frac{x_1 + x_2}{2} \right)$$

  For more help on Distance and Midpoints, see Section 6 of the Math Question Bank.

- General Linear Equations

  Know how to find your x, y coordinates and slope using this equation:
  y = b + mx

  For more help on Linear Equations, see Section 6 of the Math Question Bank.

- Absolute Value Equations

  Remember you will have two answers.

  $|x| = a$ x = -a and x = a

  Each equation must be solved separately and all solutions must be checked into the original equation.

  Example: Solve for x: $|2x - 3| = x + 1$

2x – 3 = - (x +1)	and	2x – 3 = x + 1
2x – 3 = -x – 1		
3x = 2		

  ANSWER: x = 2/3   x = 4

  For more help on Absolute Value Equations, see Section 7 of the Math Question Bank.

- Quadratics

Factoring: converting $ax^2 + bx + c$ to factored form. Find two numbers that are factors of c and whose sum is b.

Example: Factor $2x^2 + 12x + 18 = 0$

| Step 1: If possible, factor out a common monomial. | $2(x^2 - 6x + 9)$ |

Step 1: If possible, factor out a common monomial. $2(x^2 - 6x + 9)$

Step 2: Find two numbers that are factors of 9 and = -6 when added $2(x\_\_)(x\_\_)$
    -3, -3

Step 3: Fill in the binomials. Be sure to check your answer and signs. $2(x - 3)(x - 3)$

Step 4: To solve, set each to = 0.
    $x - 3 = 0$ so $x = 3$

If the equation cannot be factored (there are no two factors of c that sum to = b), the quadratic formula is used.

$$x = \frac{-b \pm \sqrt{b^2 - 4ac}}{2a}$$

Using the same equation from the above example: a = 2, b = 12, & c = 18. Plug into the formula and solve. Remember there will still be two answers due to the (+) and (-) before the radical.

You must solve for each. The following is an example of a PSAT word problem that would use a quadratic equation to solve:

The square of a number is 8 less than 6 times the number. What numbers make this statement true?

Step 1: Set up the equation. $x^2 = 6x - 8$

Step 2: Put in standard form. $x^2 - 6x + 8 = 0$

Step 3: Solve using either method. $(x - 1)(x - 8)$
    $x - 1 = 0$ $x = 1$
    $x - 8 = 0$ $x = 8$

ANSWER: x = 1,   x = 8

If the quadratic is a difference of two squares (b = 0 and $c = n^2$ for some number n), factor it into the product of a sum and a difference.
$$x^2 - n^2 = (x - n)(x + n)$$

For more help on Quadratics, see Section 7 of the Math Question Bank.

- Functions

Functions are simple if you think of them as just another substitution problem. They are basically worked the same as any other equation. Pay attention to your math, always double check your signs, and check your answer.

The following is an example of a typical function problem, followed by function rules and definitions you need to know.

If $f(x) = x^2 + 3x$, find $f(x + 2)$.

Step 1: Simply replace $(x + 2)$ for x.
$x^2 + 3x$

$(x + 2)^2 + 3(x + 2)$

Step 2: Use FOIL for first term. $\qquad x^2 + 4x + 4 + 3x + 6$

Step 3: Combine like terms. $\qquad x^2 + 7x + 10$

Step 4: Factor. $\qquad (x + 5)(x + 2)$

Step 5: Set equations to zero. Solve. $\quad x + 5 = 0 \quad$ so $x = -5$
$\qquad\qquad\qquad\qquad\qquad\qquad\qquad x + 2 = 0 \quad$ so $x = -2$

ANSWER: Solution set: $-2, -5$

Rules of Functions:

1. Adding: $(f + g)(x) = f(x) + g(x)$
   Example: If $f(x) = 3x + 2$ and $g(x) = x^2$, then $(f + g)(x) = 3x + 2 + x^2$

2. Subtracting: $(f - g)(x) = f(x) - g(x)$
   Example: If $f(x) = 3x + 2$ and $g(x) = x^2$, then $(f - g)(x) = 3x + 2 - x^2$

3. Multiplying: $(f \cdot g)(x) = f(x) \cdot g(x)$
   Example: If $f(x) = 3x + 2$ and $g(x) = x^2$, then $(f \cdot g)(x) = (3x + 2) \cdot x^2$

4. Dividing: $(f/g)(x) = f(x)/g(x)$, provided $g(x) \neq 0$

    Example: If $f(x) = 3x + 2$ and $g(x) = x^2$, then $(f/g)(x) = (3x+2)/x^2$

5. Composition: $(f \circ g)(x) = f(g(x))$

    Replace each x in the formula of $f(x)$ with the entire formula of $g(x)$.

    Example: If $f(x) = x^2 - x$ and $g(x) = x - 4$,

$(f \circ g)(x) = f(g(x))$	$(g \circ f)(x) = g(f(x))$
$= f(x-4)$	$= g(x^2 - x)$
$= (x-4)^2 - (x-4)$	$= (x^2 - x) - 4$

    (can be reduced further)

TEST SECRET

The PSAT doesn't use the typical function symbol *f(x)*; instead you will see any variety of symbols between the variables like *x*Ω*y* or *x·y* . To solve, just plug the given value into the places where their respective variables occur in the original equation:

Ex: If *x*Ω*y* = 4 – *x/y*, what is the value of *6*Ω*2*:

    4 – (6/2)   ANSWER=1

For more help on Functions, see Section 7 of the Math Question Bank.

- Geometry

    The general PSAT math section only requires knowledge of basic geometry learned through the eighth grade level. As previously mentioned, the PSAT will supply the formulas you need, but you must be able to apply them to word problems and manipulate the equations as needed. You will also need to be familiar with basic angle and shape terminology. Two typical PSAT geometry problems follow.

Acute angle:	Measures less than 90°
Acute triangle:	Each angle measures less than 90°
Obtuse angle:	Measures greater than 90°
Obtuse triangle:	One angle measures greater than 90°
Adjacent angles:	Share a side and a vertex
Complementary angles:	Adjacent angles that sum to 90°
Supplementary angles:	Adjacent angles that sum to 180°

Vertical angles:	Angles that are opposite of eachother: they are always congruent (equal in measure).
Equilateral triangle:	All angles are equal
Isosceles triangle:	Two sides and two angles are equal
Scalene:	No equal angles
Parallel lines:	Lines that will never intersect. Y ‖ X means line Y is parallel to line X
Perpendicular lines:	Lines that intersect or cross to form 90° angles
Transversal line:	A line that crosses parallel lines
Bisector:	Any line that cuts a line segment, angle, or polygon exactly in half
Polygon:	Any enclosed plane shape with three or more connecting sides (ex. a triangle)
Regular polygon:	Has all equal sides and equal angles (ex. square)
Arc:	A portion of a circle's edge
Chord:	A line segment that connects two different points on a circle
Tangent:	Something that touches a circle at only one point without crossing through it
Sum of Angles:	The sum of angles of a polygon can be calculated using $(n-1)180^\circ$ n = the number of sides

Know the names of sided plane figures:

Number of Sides and Name

3	triangle or trigon	11	hendecagon
4	quadrilateral or tetragon	12	dodecagon
5	pentagon	13	tridecagon
6	hexagon	14	tetradecagon
7	heptagon	15	pentadecagon
8	octagon	16	hexadecagon
9	nonagon	17	heptadecagon
10	decagon	18	octadecagon
Example:			

What is the area of the below square, if the length of BD is $2\sqrt{2}$?

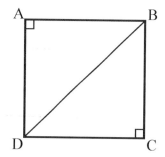

Step 1: Find the length of the side of the square in order to get the area.

Step 2: The diagonal BD makes two 45°-45°-90° triangles with the sides of the square.

Step 3: Use the 45°-45°-90° special triangle ratio $n{:}n{:}n\sqrt{2}$. If the hypotenuse is $2\sqrt{2}$ then the legs must be 2. So the length of the side of the square is 2.

Step 4: Area of square $= s^2 = 2^2 = 4$

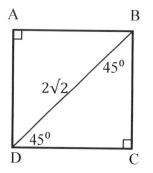

Example: In the figure below, what is the value of y?

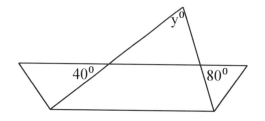

Step 1: Vertical angles are equal, so fill in two angles in the triangle that $y°$ belongs to.

Step 2: Sum of angles in a triangle = 180°.

$$\text{So, } y° + 40° + 80° = 180°$$
$$y° + 120° = 180°$$
$$y° = 60°$$

For more help on Geometry, see Section 8 of the Math Question Bank.

- Word Problems

The word problems found on the PSAT are designed such that you only need to apply the math techniques you have learned in order to solve them. So far you have seen several ways these techniques can be used, such as linear systems. The types of word problems you can expect to encounter are basic arithmetic, algebra, set and sequence, motion, work, ratio, proportion and percent.

The most important part of the word problem is setting up the equation. After that, it's a matter of plugging in the data given and solving the problem. The key to setting the problem up is knowing what the problem is asking for. The following are the general steps used to solve word problems; however, not all steps are needed for every problem. The **Check Your Knowledge** section at the end of the math chapter has samples of the various types of word problems to refresh your memory.

General Steps for Word Problem Solving:

Step 1: Determine what the problem is asking for.
Step 2: List all the given data.
Step 3: Sketch diagrams with given data.
Step 4: Determine formula(s) needed.
Step 5: Set up equation(s).
Step 6: Solve.
Step 7: Check your answer.

- Fundamental Counting Principle

  The number of possibilities of an event happening x the number of possibilities of another event happening = the total number of possibilities.

  Example: If you take a multiple-choice test with 5 questions, with 4 answer choices for each question, how many test result possibilities are there?

  Question 1 has 4 choices, question 2 has 4 choices, etc., so you have 4 x 4 x 4 x 4 x 4 (one for each question) = 1024.

  ANSWER: 1024 possible test results

  For more help on Fundamental Counting Principle, see Section 9 of the Math Question Bank.

- Probabilities

  Number of desired outcomes/Number of possible outcomes (the piece/ the whole).

  For more help on Probabilities, see Section 10 of the Math Question Bank.

Check Your Knowledge

The following set of questions represents standard PSAT problems to check your understanding of the math skills you'll need. They are in no particular order of difficulty and detailed solutions follow. Your ability to complete these questions correctly will be an indicator as to how much review is needed for each math concept.

Should you need help reviewing a specific concept, refer to the "Math Resources" section in the References and Help chapter.

Math Review Problem Set

1. John has a square piece of paper with sides that are 4 inches each. He rolled up the paper to form a cylinder. What is the volume of the cylinder?

(A) $\dfrac{4}{\pi}$

(B) $\dfrac{16}{\pi}$

(C) 16

(D) 4π

(E) 16π

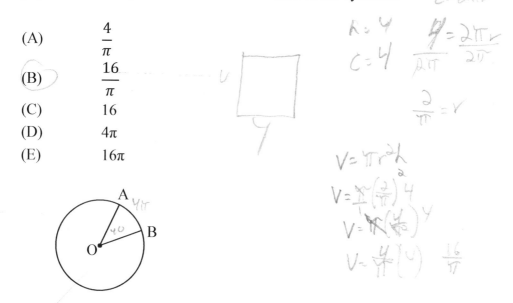

2. In the figure above, if $\angle AOB = 40°$ and the length of arc AB is 4π, what is the area of the sector AOB?

(A) 4π
(B) 16π
(C) 36π
(D) 128π
(E) 324π

3. A jet airplane and a propeller airplane pass close to each other going in opposite directions. The jet is flying four times faster than the propeller plane. After two hours of flying in opposite directions, the airplanes are 1,500 miles apart. How fast is the propeller plane flying?

(A) 750 mph
(B) 150 mph
(C) 300 mph
(D) 500 mph
(E) 200 mph

44

4. The reciprocal of $\frac{\sqrt{3}}{2}$ is:

(A) $\frac{2}{\sqrt{3}}$

(B) $\frac{3}{2}$

(C) $\frac{2\sqrt{2}}{3}$

(D) $\frac{2\sqrt{3}}{3}$

(E) $\frac{3\sqrt{2}}{2}$

5. Given that $f(x) = x^2 - 1$ and $g(x) = x + 1$, find $(f \cdot g)(x)$.

(A) $x^2 + 2x$
(B) x^2
(C) $x^3 + x^2 - x - 1$
(D) $x^3 - 1$
(E) $x^3 - x^2 + x - 1$

6. If the measure of three angles of a triangle is represented by x, $2x - 20$, and $3x - 10$, then the triangle is:

(A) Right
(B) Obtuse
(C) Acute
(D) Equilateral
(E) Isosceles

7. A bicyclist is training for a race. His training route is 75 miles. If he increases his speed by 5 mph, he could complete the course in 25 % less time. What is his average rate of speed?

(A) 11 mph
(B) 16.5 mph
(C) 15 mph
(D) 10 mph
(E) 12 mph

8. Solve for x: $4^{3x} = \dfrac{1}{8^{x-3}}$

(A)   -3

(B) $\dfrac{-3}{2}$

(C) $\dfrac{-3}{5}$

(D)   1

(E)   -1

9. Mark can paint a room in 4 hours and Chris can paint the same room in 6 hours. If Mark works alone for 1 hour and Chris helps him finish painting the room, how long will it take them if they work at their normal speeds?

(A)   2 hours
(B)   4 hours
(C)   5 hours
(D)   3 1/2 hours
(E)   1 4/5 hours

10. What is the length of a line that connects the points J (5,6) and L (2,1)?

(A) $\sqrt{34}$
(B) $\sqrt{58}$
(C)   8
(D)   14
(E)   10

11. The expression $x^{-1} + y^{-1}$ is equivalent to:

(A) $(x + y)^{-1}$

(B) $\dfrac{1}{x+y}$

(C) $x + y$

(D) $\dfrac{x+y}{xy}$

(E) $\dfrac{xy}{x+y}$

12. The roots of a quadratic equation are 3 and 1. Find the equation.

(A) $x^2 + 4x + 3 = 0$
(B) $x^2 - 4x - 3 = 0$
(C) $x^2 - 4x + 3 = 0$
(D) $x^2 - 2x - 3 = 0$
(E) $x^2 + 2x + 3 = 0$

13. If $f(x) = x + \dfrac{1}{x}$ then $f(\dfrac{1}{x}) =$

(A) $\qquad$ $x^2 + 1$

(B) $\qquad$ $f(x)$

(C) $\qquad$ $x^2 + x$

(D) $\qquad$ $\dfrac{2}{x}$

(E) $\qquad$ $\dfrac{x^2 + 1}{x^2}$

14. The sum of the digits of a two-digit number is 11. The number obtained by interchanging the digits exceeds twice the original number by 34. What is the original number?

(A) $\qquad$ 47
(B) $\qquad$ 38
(C) $\qquad$ 29
(D) $\qquad$ 56
(E) $\qquad$ 65

15. Twenty ounces of a 30% vinegar solution was mixed with 40 ounces of a 20% vinegar solution. What was the vinegar percentage of the final solution?

(A) $\qquad$ 25%
(B) $\qquad$ 24.8%
(C) $\qquad$ 23.3%
(D) $\qquad$ 30.5%
(E) $\qquad$ None of the above

16. Leslie deposits part of $3000 in a certificate of deposit (CD) that pays simple annual interest of 2.71% and the rest in a pass book savings account that pays 0.75% compounded annually. If she earns $34.26 in total interest for one year from both accounts, how much did she deposit into her savings account?

(A) $\qquad$ $220
(B) $\qquad$ $2100
(C) $\qquad$ $500
(D) $\qquad$ $2400
(E) $\qquad$ $1000

17. Two pounds (lbs.) of pears and 3 lbs. of apples cost a total of $4.26, whereas 3 lbs. of pears and 2 lbs. of apples cost $4.49. What is the per pound cost of each fruit?

(A) pears $0.76; apples $0.99
(B) pears $0.84; apples $1.09
(C) pears $0.99; apples $0.76
(D) pears $1.09; apples $0.84
(E) pears $1.09; apples $0.76

18. One room of an apartment is 12 ft. by 15 ft. The walls are 9 1/2 feet high. How much paint will you need to paint the four walls if one gallon is enough to cover 425 square feet (rounded to nearest tenth)?

(A) 1.8 gallons
(B) 2.1 gallons
(C) 1.5 gallons
(D) 1.7 gallons
(E) 1.2 gallons

19. Simplify $\sqrt{49a^3b} - \sqrt{a^3b} + 2a\sqrt{ab}$.

(A) $8a^2\sqrt{ab}$
(B) $8a\sqrt{ab}$
(C) $9a^2b^2$
(D) $8a^3b^2$
(E) $9a^2\sqrt{ab}$

20. Find the equation of the line which passes through the points (1, 6) and (-1, -2).

(A) $y - 6 = 4(x - 1)$
(B) $y + 6 = -4(x + 1)$
(C) $y - 2 = 4(x - 1)$
(D) $y - 4 = -2(x - 1)$
(E) $y + 4 = 6(x - 2)$

21. You draw a card from a standard deck of cards and then put it back. You draw a second card from the same deck. What is the probability that you pulled a face card both times?

(A) 2/104
(B) 12/104
(C) 9/104
(D) 12/169
(E) 9/169

22. What is the solution set for the equation $3 + |x - 1| = 2x$?

(A)   {2}
(B)   {2, 4/3}
(C)   {4/3, 2}
(D)   {4/3, 2}
(E)   {4/3}

23. The sum of the interior angles of a polygon is $1,980°$. How many sides does the polygon have?

(A)   13
(B)   14
(C)   15
(D)   16
(E)   17

Math Review - SOLUTIONS

1. Answer: (B)

Step 1: The edge of the paper will form the circumference of the base of the cylinder.

$$C = 2\pi r = 4 \rightarrow r = \frac{4}{2\pi} \rightarrow r = \frac{2}{\pi}$$

Step 2: Volume of cylinder = area of base × height.

$$Area\ of\ base = \pi r^2 = \pi\left(\frac{2}{\pi}\right)^2 = \pi\frac{4}{\pi^2} = \frac{4}{\pi}$$

Height = edge of the paper = 4

$$Volume\ of\ cylinder = \frac{4}{\pi} \times 4 = \frac{16}{\pi}$$

2. Answer: (C)

Step 1: Arc $AB = 40°$. Circumference of circle = 360°.
Let C = circumference of circle.

$$\frac{Arc\ AB}{C} = \frac{40}{360} = \frac{1}{9}$$
$$\Rightarrow Arc\ AB = \frac{1}{9} \times C$$

Step 2: You are given that arc $AB = 4\pi$. Plug into above equation.

$$\frac{1}{9} \times C = 4\pi \Rightarrow C = 36\pi$$

Step 3: Use the formula for the circumference of circle: $C = 2\pi r$. Plug into the above equation.

$2\pi r = 36\pi$
$2r = 36$
$r = 18$

Step 4: Use the formula for the area of circle: $A = \pi r^2$. Plug in value for r.

$A = \pi(18)^2 = 324\pi$

Step 5: Sector AOB is $\frac{1}{9}$ of the area of the circle.

Sector AOB = $\frac{1}{9} \times 324\pi = 36\pi$

3. Answer: (B)

Step 1: Given data: The total distance is 1,500 miles which is equal to the distance the jet flies plus the distance the propeller plane flies. We are also told the jet (J) flies 4 times faster than the propeller plane (P). The time for both planes is 2 hours.

Step 2: Set up formulas. Remember all motion problems use the standard
$D = R \times T$; D = distance, R = rate, and T = time.
$D_{total} = D_{jet} + D_{propeller}$ $D_{jet} = (4P)(2)$ $D_{propeller} = (P)(2)$

Step 3: Solve.

$1500 = (4P)(2) + (P)(2)$
$1500 = 8P + 2P$
$1500 = 10P$
$150 = P$ The propeller plane is traveling 150 mph.

4. Answer: (D)

The reciprocal of $\frac{\sqrt{3}}{2}$ is $\frac{2}{\sqrt{3}}$, but this is not the final answer. Remember, if a denominator contains a radical, it must be rationalized, so:

$$\frac{2}{\sqrt{3}} \times \frac{\sqrt{3}}{\sqrt{3}} = \frac{2\sqrt{3}}{3}$$

5. Answer: (C)

Step 1: Set up the equation. $(f \cdot g)(x) = f(x) \cdot g(x)$
Step 2: Solve using FOIL. $(x^2 - 1)(x + 1)$

First $x^2 \cdot x = x^3$
Outer $x^2 \cdot 1 = x^2$
Inner $-1 \cdot x = -x$
Last $-1 \cdot 1 = -1$
                       $= x^3 + x^2 - x - 1$

6. Answer: (B)

The sum of all the angles of a triangle equals $180°$, so

$(x) + (2x - 20) - (3x - 10) = 180$
$6x - 30 = 180$
$6x = 210$ $x = 35$
$2x - 20 = 50$
$3x - 10 = 95$ The triangle is obtuse.

7. Answer: (C)

Step 1: Given data: The total distance is 75 miles. He has an increase in speed of 5 mph that will decrease his completion time by 25%.

Step 2: This is a motion problem, so the formula used is D = R x T.

Step 3: Set up equations. Assign x for rate and y for time.

Original $\quad x \cdot y = 75$

New $\quad (x + 5)(3/4\ y) = 75$

(1/4 of completion time saved)

Step 4: Solve. There are two equations so use system of equations.

$$(x + 5)(3/4\ y) = 75 \quad \rightarrow \quad 3/4\ xy + 15/4\ y = 75$$
$$3xy + 15y = 300$$
Substitute $xy = 75 \qquad 3(75) + 15y = 300$
$$225 + 15y = 300$$
$$15y = 75$$
$$y = 5$$

It took 5 hours to go 75 miles, so the average speed = 75/5 = 15 mph

8. Answer: (D)

Step 1: Eliminate the denominator.

Step 2: Find a common base and solve.

$$4^{3x} = \frac{1}{8^{x-3}} \quad \rightarrow \quad 4^{3x} = 8^{-(x-3)}$$
$$4^{3x} = 8^{3-x}$$
$$(2^2)^{3x} = (2^3)^{3-x}$$
$$2^{6x} = 2^{9-3x}$$
$$6x = 9 - 3x$$
$$9x = 9$$
$$x = 1$$

9. Answer: (E)

Step 1: Gather data. Mark: 1 room every 4 hrs. Chris: 1 room every 6 hrs. Mark works 1 hr alone.

Step 2: This is still a form of motion problem; R x T = Total Work. Since Chris is joining after Mark starts, let him represent x.

Step 3: Set up equations and solve.

	Chris	Mark
Rate (room/hr.):	1/6	1/4
Time:	x	$1 + x$

$$(1/6x) + (1 + x)/4 = 1 \text{ (room)}$$

$$\text{LCD} = 12 \qquad 3 + 3x + 2x = 12$$
$$5x = 9$$
$$x = 9/5 = 1\ 4/5 \text{ hrs.}$$

10. Answer: (B)

Use the distance formula. $d = \sqrt{(x_2 - x_1)^2 + (y_2 - y_1)^2}$

(5, 6) and (2, - 1) $d = \sqrt{(5 - 2)^2 + (6 - (-1))^2}$
$d = \sqrt{9 + 49} = \sqrt{58}$

11. Answer: (D)

$x^{-1} + y^{-1} \rightarrow \frac{1}{x} + \frac{1}{y} \rightarrow \frac{x}{xy} + \frac{y}{xy} \rightarrow \frac{x+y}{xy}$

12. Answer: (C)

If the roots are 3 and 1 then $x - 3 = 0$ and $x - 1 = 0$, then:
$(x - 3)(x - 1)$ FOIL $\rightarrow x^2 - x - 3x + 3 \rightarrow x^2 - 4x + 3$

13. Answer: (B)

$f(x) = x + \frac{1}{x}$ then $f(\frac{1}{x}) = \frac{1}{x} + \frac{1}{\frac{1}{x}} = \frac{1}{x} + x = f(x)$

14. Answer: (C)

$x + y = 11$
$(10y + x) = 2(10x + y) + 34$
$10y + x = 20x + 2y + 34$

Combine like terms and rearrange. $8y - 19x = 34$

Use system of equations to solve. $x + y = 11$
(multiply by $- 8$) $\rightarrow$ $-8x - 8y = -88$

$8y - 19x = 34$
$+ \quad -8y - 8x = - 88$
$\overline{\quad - 27x = - 54 \quad}$ $x = 2$

Since $x + y = 11$ and $x = 2$, y then $= 9$. The number is 29.

15. Answer: (C)

The portion amount times strength equals the total amount of solution. The percentage must be changed to decimal form before solving.

$20 \cdot 0.30 = 6$ oz.
$40 \cdot 0.20 = 8$ oz.
$60 \cdot x$ (%) $= 14$ oz.   Equation: $60(x\%) = 14$
$60/100x = 14$(percent rule piece/whole)
$x = 1400/60$
$x = 23.3\%$

16. Answer: (D)

Assume she deposited x dollars in her savings account, then she must have deposited $3000 - x$ into her CD.

Set up a table.

	Investment	Percent	Interest
	x	0.75	$0.0075x$
	$3000 - x$	2.71	$(3000 - x)0.0271$
Total	3000		34.26

Equation:
Combine like terms

$$0.0075x + (3000 - x)(0.0271) = 34.26$$
$$81.3 - 34.26 = 0.0271x - 0.0075x$$
$$47.04 = 0.0196x$$
$$2400 = x$$

17. Answer: (C)

Since there are two unknowns, you need two equations and therefore, two tables.

	Item	lb.	cost/lb.	Total cost
1st	Pears	2	x	$2x$
	Apples	3	y	$3y$
	Total cost			$2x + 3y = \$4.26$

	Item	lb.	cost/lb.	Total cost
2nd	Pears	3	x	$3x$
	Apples	2	y	$2y$
	Total cost			$3x + 2y = \$4.49$

Use system of equations.

$2x + 3y = \$4.26$ (multiply by 2)
$$4x + 6y = 8.52$$
$3x + 2y = \$4.49$ (multiply by 3)
$$9x + 6y = 13.47$$

Subtract the first equation from the second.

$$5x = 4.95$$
$$x = 0.99$$

Plug x value into original equation.

$$2(0.99) + 3y = 4.26$$
$$3y = 2.28$$
$$y = 0.76$$

Pears are $0.99 per lb.
Apples are $0.76 per lb.

18. Answer: (E)

There are four walls, two are 12 ft by 9.5 ft and two are 15 ft by 9.5 ft. so the total area is:

$$2(12 \times 9.5) + 2(15 \times 9.5) = 513 \text{ square feet. Now set up a ratio.}$$

$$\frac{1\ gal}{425\ sq.ft.} = \frac{x}{513\ sq.ft.} \rightarrow 513 = 425x \rightarrow x = 513/425 \rightarrow x = 1.2 \text{ (rounded)}$$

19. Answer: (B)

Simplify each term then put them together.

$$\sqrt{49a^3b} = \sqrt{49}\sqrt{a^2}\sqrt{ab} = 7a\sqrt{ab}$$
$$-\sqrt{a^3b} = -\sqrt{a^2}\sqrt{ab} = -a\sqrt{ab}$$
$$7a\sqrt{ab} - a\sqrt{ab} + 2a\sqrt{ab} = 8a\sqrt{ab}$$

20. Answer: (A)

To find m: $\dfrac{y_2 - y_1}{x_2 - x_1}$ points are (1, 6) and (-1, -2) so, $\dfrac{6-(-2)}{1-(-1)} = 4$

Equation of a line is: $(y - y_2) = m(x - x_1)$
Using first point: $(y - 6) = 4(x - 1)$

21. Answer: (E)

There are three face cards of each suit (4 suits) in a standard deck of 52 cards. The probability of picking one face card is then 12/52, or 3/13. The probability of picking first one face card and then another would then be:

$$3/13 \times 3/13 = 9/169$$

22. Answer: (A)

There will be two answers. Remember both answers must be checked to make sure they are valid solutions.

$$3 + |x - 1| = 2x$$
$$|x - 1| = 2x - 3$$

$-(x - 1) = 2x - 3$ $\qquad$ $x - 1 = 2x - 3$
$-x + 1 = 2x - 3$ $\qquad\qquad$ $2 = x$
$4 = 3x$
$4/3 = x$

Check: $\quad 3 + |4/3 - 1| = 2(4/3)$ $\qquad$ $3 + |2 - 1| = 2(2)$
$3 + |1/3| = 8/3$ $\qquad\qquad$ $3 + |1| = 4$
$10/3 \neq 8/3$ so 4/3 is not a solution $\qquad$ $4 = 4$ solution

23. Answer: (A)

$$(n - 2)(180) = 1980$$
$$n - 2 = 11$$
$$n = 13$$

Chapter 4: The Critical Reading Section

The critical reading and writing sections of the PSAT are often referred to as the PSAT verbal. There are two 25-minute sections and one 20-minute section, which constitute one-third of your PSAT score. There are two general types of questions that appear in the Critical Reading section: sentence completion and reading comprehension.

Sentence Completion

You have been answering these types of questions since you learned to read and write. Different forms of sentence completion questions are used for tests and quizzes in all subject areas, which is one of the reasons they are used on the PSAT; these questions test your vocabulary and ability to understand sentence structure. Each sentence contains one or more blanks, which you must fill by choosing the most appropriate words from the answer choices. Vocabulary is the primary focus. You are not expected to know every word in the English language, but you are expected to know a good percentage of commonly tested words.

Tips:

1. Read the sentence through entirely and say "blank" when you come upon one. This will give you not only a feel of the language being used, but also helps you identify any context clues, including words that lead to a transition, introductory phrases, positive reaffirmations, or negative comparisons. Transitional and introductory words are very important as they tell you the relationship between the parts of the sentence, including whether they contradict or complement each other.

2. Most students will memorize a thousand new words and their definitions and still score poorly on this section. This is because you aren't given a definition to match with a word; rather you are being tested on how it is being used in a sentence. In order to maximize your score, you must practice using the words you are learning in sentences, whether by writing, conversing, or both (highly recommended). This allows the words to become familiar to you. One way to study for this section, especially as a group, is to write down 20 new words at the beginning of the week. By the end of the week, you must use all the words on the list in a comprehensive paragraph. (This also helps with the writing section.)

3. Learn the meanings of common word prefixes, suffixes, and root words. If words appear that you don't recognize, most of the time you can deduce their meaning by examining their prefix, suffix or root.

4. Read the sentence and answer choices carefully. As sentences increase in difficulty, so does the structure of the sentence. Unnecessary errors are made when the reader fails to pay attention to the transitions and answers that would have been correct if the sentence hadn't changed direction and asked for the opposite.

5. Reread the sentence with your answer choice as a check; does it sound right?

6. If you are still unsure, try to narrow it down to a couple answer choices and make an educated guess.

Try this using the following example question taken from collegeboard.com:

There is no doubt that Sheryl is a _____: she excels at telling stories that captivate her listeners.

(A) braggart
(B) dilettante
(C) pilferer
(D) prevaricator
(E) raconteur

The answer is (E)

Vocabulary Words

There are no lists of vocabulary words in this book. As mentioned earlier, you need to actively learn more words by coming up with games, working with other students, using flash cards, and any combination thereof. You must learn the words, and then apply them for their meaning to be understood. Reading words from a book is probably the least effective method possible. Please see the "References and Help" chapter on page 71 of this book for places to find help and improve your vocabulary.

TEST SECRET

Don't memorize thousands of words! The PSAT does not test definitions of words. Improve your general vocabulary and become familiar with the meaning of words, not their verbatim definitions.

Reading Comprehension

In this section, you will be presented with various texts, ranging from 100 to 800 words in length, to read and then answer questions. The test measures your ability to comprehend the passage, as well as your ability to reason about the subject of the passage. There are three types of basic questions you will encounter:

1. Vocabulary in context – you are asked to give the author intended meaning of the word. Caution: in many cases, the words have meanings different from a dictionary definition, so make sure you are choosing the author's intended meaning.

2. Literal comprehension questions which simply ask for what the passage is stating.

3. Extended reasoning – most of the questions are of this type. These are questions such as: What was the author's tone? What is being inferred? What is the main point?

Tips:

1. When there is an opportunity, read the passage with subject matter that is of interest or familiar to you first, even if it happens to be the last reading passage.

2. Pay attention to how the paragraphs begin and end. PSAT passages are written in general English prose, meaning you'll find the topic sentence at the very beginning of the passage and main point commonly in the ending sentence(s). You can then skim the material in-between.

3. Make short notes beside certain passages to mark important information so it's easier to find if you need to return.

4. Unless the answer comes immediately to mind, save the more detailed questions for last as they tend to require you to return to the passage. Answering the general questions first will maximize your points.

5. All the answers will come from the passage, either directly or indirectly. Don't use any previous knowledge you have on the subject – only draw from the passage read on the test.

6. Although you can decide what order you want to read the passages, don't move to another section until you have answered all of the questions you can on the passage just read. Chances are if you leave a passage before completing all that you can, you will have to reread the passage later, which is a time killer.

7. An answer choice can appear to be true and still be the wrong answer. The correct answer will be the one that best answers the question according to the passage; therefore, an answer choice can be factually true but not necessarily correct.

8. If you are still unsure, make your best educated guess if you can narrow your answer choices down.

9. Practice! The only way to improve is to spend time to practicing critical reading.

Below is an example of a typical Reading Comprehension sample you might see on the PSAT, followed by three questions. Use this as a chance to practice your understanding of the above outlined concepts, and check your answers when you are done.

Example of Reading Comprehension:

He Had His Dream

(1) He had his dream, and all through life,
Worked up to it through toil and strife.
Afloat fore'er before his eyes,
It colored for him all his skies:
(5) The storm-cloud dark
Above his bark,
The calm and listless vault of blue
Took on its hopeful hue,
It tinctured every passing beam—
(10) He had his dream.
He labored hard and failed at last,
His sails too weak to bear the blast,
The raging tempests tore away
And sent his beating bark astray.
(15) But what cared he
For wind or sea!
He said, "The tempest will be short,
My bark will come to port."
He saw through every cloud a gleam—
(20) He had his dream.

~ Paul Laurence Dunbar

1. What is the meaning of the word bark in lines 6, 14, and 18?

a. heart
b. storm
c. ocean
d. tree
e. boat

2. Which of the following is true about the form of the poem?

a. Almost every pair of lines rhymes, and all have the same rhythm pattern.
b. The poem has two stanzas, and each follows the same rhyme and rhythm pattern.
c. The poem has no rhyming lines and no regular rhythm pattern.
d. Every other line of each stanza rhymes and has the same rhythm pattern.
e. Every pair of lines rhymes, but there is no regular rhythm pattern.

3. Which of these sayings best expresses the message of this poem?

a. A bird in the hand is worth two in the bush.
b. A friend in need is a friend indeed.
c. Necessity is the mother of invention.
d. Keep your mind on your goal and never give up.
e. Wishing won't make it so.

Answers:

1. **e.**
The context of the poem makes it clear that "bark" here means boat or ship. The images of the first and second stanza depict a boat that is tossed and battered by a storm.

2. **b.**
The poem is divided into two stanzas that follow the same pattern. Pairs of lines rhyme, but the rhythms vary from couplet to couplet so choices a, c, and d are incorrect. Although the rhythms vary from couplet to couplet, each stanza follows the same rhythmic pattern, making choice e incorrect as well. Choice b is the correct answer.

3. **d.**
The poem describes how having a dream helped a man maintain optimism in the face of challenges. The saying that best expresses this idea is choice d. Choice e is precisely the opposite of this idea. Choice a means that one should be satisfied with what one can attain, which also goes against the theme of striving against all odds. Choices b and c have nothing to do with the content of the poem.

Chapter 5: The Writing Section

The multiple-choice questions include error identification questions, sentence improvement questions, and paragraph improvement questions. Identifying sentence errors tests your ability to recognize errors in usage and to recognize effective sentence structure. Sentence improvement questions test your ability to correct usage and structure errors. Paragraph improvement questions test your ability to revise sentences in the context of a paragraph or the entire essay, as well as organize and develop paragraphs in a coherent and logical manner.

Example of Sentence Improvement:

The following is a sample of sentence improvement questions you will encounter on the PSAT. Carefully read and answer these questions, and then check your answers afterwards. If you find that you are struggling with the examples below and need more help, you can find more practice questions to sharpen your skills in the Accepted, Inc. Critical Reading & Writing Question Bank.

A

(1) Of the two types of eclipses, the most common is the lunar eclipse, which occurs when a full moon passes through Earth's shadow. (2) The disc-shaped moon slowly disappears completely or turns a coppery red color. (3) Solar and lunar eclipses both occur from time to time.

B

(4) During a solar eclipse, the moon passes between the Earth and Sun. (5) As the moon moves into alignment, it blocks the light from the Sun creating an eerie darkness. (6) When the moon is perfectly in position, the Sun's light is visible as a ring, or corona, around the dark disc of the moon. (7) A lunar eclipse can be viewed from anywhere on the nighttime half of Earth, a solar eclipse can only be viewed from a zone that is only about 200 miles wide and covers about one-half of a percent of Earth's total area.

1. Sentence 1: Of the two types of eclipses, the most common is the lunar eclipse, which occurs when a full moon passes through Earth's shadow. What correction should be made to this sentence?

a. Change most to more.
b. Change occurs to occur.
c. Change which to that.
d. Change Earth's to Earths'.
e. No correction is necessary.

2. Sentence 2: The disc-shaped moon slowly disappears completely or turns a coppery red color. If you rewrote sentence 2, beginning with <u>The disc-shaped moon slowly turns a coppery red color,</u> the next word should be:

a. and
b. but
c. when
d. because
e. or

3. Which revision would improve the effectiveness of paragraph A?

a. Remove sentence 1.
b. Move sentence 2 to the beginning of the paragraph.
c. Remove sentence 2.
d. Move sentence 3 to the beginning of the paragraph.
e. No revision is necessary.

4. Sentence 7: A lunar eclipse can be viewed from anywhere on the nighttime half of Earth, a solar eclipse can only be viewed from a zone that is only about 200 miles wide and covers about one-half of a percent of Earth's total area. Which of the following is the best way to write the underlined portion of this sentence? If the original is the best way, choose option **a**.

a. Earth, a solar eclipse
b. Earth a solar eclipse
c. Earth; a solar eclipse
d. Earth, because a solar eclipse
e. Earth, when a solar eclipse

Answers:

1. **a.**
Use the comparative when comparing only two things. Here, you are comparing two types of eclipses, so more is correct. The other changes introduce errors.

2. **e.**
The clauses are joined by the conjunction or in the original sentence. Maintaining this conjunction maintains the original relationship between ideas.

3. **d.**
Placing sentence 3 at the beginning of the paragraph would make the paragraph more effective because sentence 3 makes a good topic sentence. It also leads directly into sentence 1.

4. **c.**
The two related sentences should be separated by a semicolon. The other answers suggest incorrect punctuation or introduce inaccurate relationships between the sentences.

Chapter 6: Resources and Help

If you read through some of this book and thought, "Uh oh...I don't really remember learning that," that's ok! You are not alone. There is a good chance you are feeling this way about the math section since that is where most students find they have forgotten some material. Not to worry, below is a list of resources for additional help.

Math Resources

Purple Math   www.purplemath.com

Purple math is a fantastic resource for intensive help on individual mathematic concepts. The website offers many extended tutorials in each of the subjects listed in the math section of this book. Practice questions are available here, so use them if you need more opportunities to improve.

Khan Academy   www.khanacademy.org

Khan Academy is a great resource for reviewing PSAT math questions, as well as tutorials related to individual concepts listed in this book. Simply visit the website and scroll down to the concepts you want to learn about. Click on the "Test Prep" button and then select "PSAT Math" in the drop down bar to reach a large section of PSAT math questions. There, you can follow along with the tutorial as every single question is worked out step by step!

Flash Cards

While flash cards don't work for full PSAT word problems, they can be valuable for improving your mental math abilities. Accepted, Inc. offers "brain trainer" math flash-cards to work on speed and accuracy in answering basic math questions. Flash cards help improve your mental math ability, as well as review concepts you must be familiar with for success on the exam. Visit our website under the Product menu to find the cards.

Practice Questions

Working through practice questions is a great way to figure out what you need to improve on and to solidify your understanding of individual concepts. We have included in this book a question bank of approximately 150 individual questions, divided into sections by concept (see page 81). Work through them all to practice everything, or you can easily pick out the specific concepts where you need improvement.

Critical Reading and Writing Resources

Vocabulary, by nature, requires more work. Unlike math, review and practice problems won't get you the same results, so you have to find a way to study and learn what works for you. Do not simply read through lists of words. Instead, make your practice interactive as noted in the critical reading chapter.

www.freevocabulary.com
This great website offers over 5,000 PSAT vocabulary words and is a good place to review and find words you do NOT know immediately. There is no need to memorize all 5,000 words! Instead, cull out words you already know and focus on improving and expanding your vocabulary.

www.vocabulary.com
This website offers interactive "challenges" to learn words and improve your vocabulary, and is a great place to find definitions, if needed. You will also find multiple lists of PSAT words that you are likely to encounter on the exam.

Practice Questions
Just like with the math section, we have included in this book a bank of 150 practice questions for the writing and critical reading section. Practice essays are included.

Flash Cards
Many people find that flashcards are a quick and easy way to actively learn more words. Accepted, Inc. has high-yield flashcards with the top PSAT words as well as roots, prefixes, and suffixes you need to know for the exam.

Other Resources

You've probably had at least one really great teacher that you liked and trusted. Even if you took their class years ago, such teachers can still be a great resource! Also, even if they didn't teach the specific course with which you need help, don't count them out. Science teachers are proficient in math, and history teachers have a background in writing. If nothing else, they can help you find more resources who can help. Remember, the PSAT is only testing what you have been taught through high school, and all these teachers went through advanced courses in these subjects during college.

Chapter 7: Math Question Bank

Section 1: Percent/Part/Whole, Percent Change, Repeated Percent Change, Simple Interest

1) If an account is opened with a starting balance of $500, what is the amount in the account after 3 years if the account pays simple interest of 5%?

A) $565
B) $570
C) $575
D) $545
E) $540

2) In a class of 42 students, 18 are boys. Two girls get transferred to another school. What percent of students remaining are girls?

A) 14%
B) 16%
C) 52.4%
D) 60%
E) None of the above

3) A payroll check is issued for $500.00. If 20% goes to bills, 30% of the remainder goes to pay entertainment expenses, 10% of what is left is placed in a retirement account, then approximately how much is remaining?

A) $150
B) $250
C) $170
D) $350
E) $180

4) A painting by Van Gogh increased in value by 80% from year 1995 to year 2000. If in year 2000, the painting is worth $7200, what was its value in 1995?

A) $1500
B) $2500
C) $3000
D) $4000
E) $5000

5) 'Dresses and Ties' sells a frilly dress for $60 dollars. But they decide to discount the price of that dress by 25%. How much does the dress cost now?

A) $55
B) $43
C) $45
D) $48
E) $65

6) I deposit $1000 in a savings account that pays 3% simple interest. How much will I get after five years?

A) $1200
B) $2500
C) $1500
D) $1150
E) None of the above

7) A sweater goes on sale for 30% off. If the original price of the sweater was $70, what is the discounted price?

A) $48
B) $49
C) $51
D) $65
E) $52

8) If the value of a car depreciates by 60% over ten years and its value in the year 2000 is $2500, what was its value in the year 1990?

A) $6000
B) $6230
C) $6250
D) $6500
E) $6600

9) If an account is opened with a starting balance of $500, what is the amount in the account after 3 years if the account pays compound interest of 5%?

A) $560.80
B) $578.81
C) $564.50
D) $655.10
E) $660.00

10) A piece of memorabilia depreciates by 1% every year. If the value of the memorabilia is $75000, what will it be 2 years from now? Give the answer as a whole number.

   A) $74149
   B) $74150
   C) $73151
   D) $71662
   E) $73507

11) A dress is marked down by 20% in an effort to boost sales for one week. After that week the price of the dress is brought back to the original value. What percent did the price of the dress have to be increased from its discounted price?

   A) 20%
   B) 25%
   C) 120%
   D) 125%
   E) 15%

12) A car dealer increases the price of a car by 30%, but then discounts it by 30%. What is the relationship between the final price and the original price?

   A) .91x : x
   B) .98x : x
   C) 1:1
   D) .88x : x
   E) .75x : x

#1 Solution
Answer: C
Amount = P(1+rT) = 500(1+.05*3) = 575
Skill: Simple Interest

#2 Solution
Answer: None of the above.
The entire class has 42 students, of which 18 are boys, meaning 42-18 = 24 is the number of girls. Out of these 24 girls, two leave, so 22 girls are left. But the total number of students is now 42-2 = 40.
22/40 * 100 = 55%
Reminder: If you forget to subtract two from the total number of students you will end up with 60% as the answer. Although you may calculate an answer that has been given as a choice, it doesn't mean that it is correct. Always check your answer.
Skill: Percent/Part/Whole

#3 Solution
Answer: B
If out of the entire paycheck, 20% is first taken out, the remainder is 80%. Of this remainder, if 30% is used for entertainment, then (.8-.80*.30) = .560 is left. If 10% is put into a retirement account, then (.56- .56*.1) = .504 is remaining. So out of $500, the part that remains is 50%, which is $252.
Skill: Percent/Part/Whole

#4 Solution
Answer: D
In 2005, the value was 1.8 times its value in 1995. So 1.8x = 7200→x = 4000
Skill: Percent/Part/Whole

#5 Solution
Answer: C
60 * (100-25)/100 → 60*.75 = 45.
Skill: Percent Change

#6 Solution
Answer: D
Using the formula A = P*(1+r*t), we get A = 1000*(1+.03*5)→A = 1150.
Skill: Simple Interest

#7 Solution
Answer: B
New price = original price *(1-discount)→new price = 70(1-.3)= 49.
Skill: Percent Change

#8 Solution
Answer: C

$Value_{2000}$ = Original price*$(1-.6) \rightarrow 2500 = .4P = 2500 \rightarrow P = 6250$.

Skill: Percent Change

#9 Solution
Answer: B

Amount = $P(1+r)^t = 500*1.05^3 = \$578.81$.

Skill: Compound Interest

#10 Solution
Answer: E

Final value = $75000(1-.1)^2 = 73507$.

Skill: Repeated Percent Change

#11 Solution
Answer: B

If the original price of the dress was x, then the discounted price would be 0.8x. To increase the price from .8x to x, the percent increase would be $(x-.8x)/.8x * 100 = 25\%$.

Skill: Percent/Part/Whole

12 Solution
Answer: A

Let the original price of the car be x. Then, after the 30% increase, the price is 1.3x. After discounting the increased price by 30%, it now is $.7*1.3x = .91x$.

Therefore, the ratio of the final price to the original price = $.91x : x$.

Skill: Percentage and Ratio

Section 2: Mean, Median, Mode, Combined Averages

1) If test A is taken 5 times with an average result of 21, and test B is taken 13 times with an average result of 23, what is the combined average?

- A) 22.24
- B) 22.22
- C) 22.00
- D) 22.44
- E) 24.22

2) A set of data has 12 entries. The average of the first 6 entries is 12, the average of the next two entries is 20, and the average of the remaining entries is 4. What is the average of the entire data set?

- A) 10
- B) 10.67
- C) 11
- D) 12.67
- E) 10.5

3) What is the average score of 8 tests where the score for 3 tests is 55, the score for two tests is 35 and the remaining tests have scores of 70?

- A) 50.3
- B) 52.5
- C) 55.1
- D) 56.0
- E) 55.6

4) The temperatures over a week are recorded as follows:

Day	High	Low
Monday	80	45
Tuesday	95	34
Wednesday	78	47
Thursday	79	55
Friday	94	35
Saturday	67	46
Sunday	76	54

What is the approximate average high temperature and average low temperature during the week?

A) 90,50
B) 80,40
C) 81,45
D) 82,46
E) 81,47

5) Twelve teams competed in a mathematics test. The scores recorded for each team are: 29, 30, 28, 27, 35, 43, 45, 50, 46, 37, 44, 41. What is the median score?

A) 37
B) 41
C) 39
D) 44
E) 45

6) A class of 10 students scores 90, 78, 45, 98, 84, 79, 66, 87, 78, 94. What is the mean score? What is the median score? What is the mode?

A) 69.9, 81.5, 78
B) 79.9, 80, 78
C) 79.9, 87, 76
D) Not enough information given
E) None of the above

7) A shop sells 3 kinds of t-shirts: one design sells for $4.50, the second design sells for $13.25 and the third design sells for $15.50. If the shop sold 8 shirts of the first design, 12 shirts of the second design and 4 shirts of the third design, what was the average selling price of the shirts?

A) $10.71
B) $10.25
C) $14.55
D) $12.55
E) $5.80

#1 Solution
Answer: D
If test A avg = 21 for 5 tests, then sum of test A results = 21*5 = 105.
If test B avg = 23 for 13 tests, then sum of test B results = 23*13 = 299.
So total result = 299+105 = 404.
Average of all tests = 404/(5+13) = 404/18 = 22.44.
Skill: Combined Averages

#2 Solution
Answer: B
The average of the first 6 points is 12→ $s_1/6 = 12$→$s_1 = 72$; s_1 is the sum of the first 6 points.
The average of the next 2 points is 20→$s_2/2 = 20$→$s_2 = 40$; s_2 is the sum of the next 2 points.
The average of the remaining 4 pts is 4→$s_3/4 = 4$→$s_3 = 16$; s_3 is the sum of the last 4 points.
The sum of all the data points = 72+40+16 = 128.
The average = 128/12 = 10.67.
Skill: Mean, Median, Mode

#3 Solution
Answer: E
Average = (3*55+2*35+3*70)/8→Average = 55.625.
Skill: Combined Averages

#4 Solution
Answer:C
Average of high s= (80+95+78+79+94+67+76)/7 = 81.29.
Average of low s= (45+34+47+55+35+46+54)/7 = 45.14.
Skill: Mean, Median, Mode

#5 Solution
Answer: C
To find the median, we first have to put the list in order:
27, 28, 29, 30, 35, 37, 41, 43, 44, 45, 46, 50.
The middle two scores are 37 and 41, and their average is 39
Skill: Mean, Median, Mode

#6 Solution
Answer: None of the above
The mean is just the total score/number of scores→90+....+94)/10→79.9
The median is the score located in the middle. The middle of the set of the numbers is between 84 and 79→Find the average of these two scores: 81.5
The mode is the number that occurs the most: 78
Skill: Mean, Median, Mode

<u>#7 Solution</u>
Answer: A
Multiply each t-shirt price with the number sold, add them together and divide by the total number of shirts sold.
So Average Price = (4.50*8 + 13.25*12 + 15.50*4)/(8+12+4)→Average = $10.71.
Skill: Combined Averages

Section 3: Exponents & Roots

1) What is $x^2y^3z^5/y^2z^{-9}$?

    A) y^5z^4
    B) yz^4
    C) x^2yz^{14}
    D) $x^2y^5z^4$
    E) xyz

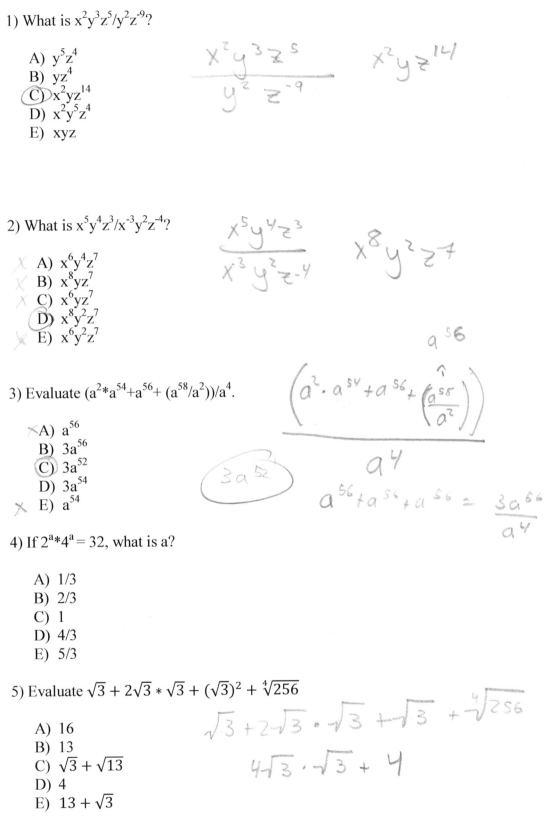

2) What is $x^5y^4z^3/x^{-3}y^2z^{-4}$?

    A) $x^6y^4z^7$
    B) x^8yz^7
    C) x^6yz^7
    D) $x^8y^2z^7$
    E) $x^6y^2z^7$

3) Evaluate $(a^2*a^{54}+a^{56}+ (a^{58}/a^2))/a^4$.

    A) a^{56}
    B) $3a^{56}$
    C) $3a^{52}$
    D) $3a^{54}$
    E) a^{54}

4) If $2^a*4^a = 32$, what is a?

    A) 1/3
    B) 2/3
    C) 1
    D) 4/3
    E) 5/3

5) Evaluate $\sqrt{3} + 2\sqrt{3} * \sqrt{3} + (\sqrt{3})^2 + \sqrt[4]{256}$

    A) 16
    B) 13
    C) $\sqrt{3} + \sqrt{13}$
    D) 4
    E) $13 + \sqrt{3}$

#1 Solution

Answer: C

$x^2y^3z^5/y^2z^{-9} = x^2y^3z^5 * y^{-2}z^9$ which gives the answer $x^2y^{(3-2)}z^{(5+9)} \rightarrow x^2yz^{14}$

Skill: Exponents

#2 Solution

Answer: D

$x^5y^4z^3/x^{-3}y^2z^{-4} = x^5y^4z^3 * x^3y^{-2}z^4 = x^8y^2z^7$

Skill: Exponents

#3 Solution

Answer: C

$(a^2*a^{54}+a^{56}+ (a^{58}/a^2))/a^4 = (a^{54+2}+a^{56}+a^{58-2})a^{-4} = 3a^{56}-4 = 3a^{52}$

Skill: Exponents

#4 Solution

Answer: E

2^a*4^a can be re written as $2^a*(2^2)^a$.

$32 = 2^5$.

Therefore, $2^{(a+2a)} = 2^5 \rightarrow 3a = 5 \rightarrow a = 5/3$.

Skill: Exponents

#5 Solution

Answer: E

This evaluates to $\sqrt{3} + 6 + 3 + 4$ which is $13+\sqrt{3}$.

Skill: Roots

Section 4: Algebraic Equations

1) The number 568cd should be divisible by 2, 5, and 7. What are the values for c and d?

    A) 56835
    B) 56830
    C) 56860
    D) 56840
    E) 56800

2) Carla is 3 times older than her sister Megan. Eight years ago Carla was 18 years older than her sister. What is Megan's age?

    A) 10
    B) 8
    C) 9
    D) 6
    E) 5

3) What is the value of $f(x) = (x^2-25)/(x+5)$ when $x = 0$?

    A) -1
    B) -2
    C) -3
    D) -4
    E) -5

4) Four years from now, John will be twice as old as Sally will be. If Sally was 10 eight years ago, how old is John?

    A) 35
    B) 40
    C) 45
    D) 50
    E) 55

5) I have some marbles. I give 25% to Vic, 20% to Robbie, 10% to Jules, then I give 6/20 of the remaining amount to my brother, and keep the rest for myself. If I end up with 315 marbles, how many did I have to begin with?

    A) 1000
    B) 1500

C) 3500
D) 400
E) 500

6) I have some marbles. I give 25% to Vic, 20% of the remainder to Robbie, 10% of that remainder to Jules and me, then I give 6/20 of the remaining amount to my brother, and keep the rest for myself. If I end up with 315 marbles, how many did I have to begin with?

    A) 800
    B) 833
    C) 834
    D) 378
    E) 500

7) If $x = 5y+4$, what is the value of y if $x = 29$?

    A) 33/5
    B) 5.5
    C) 5
    D) 0
    E) 29/5

8) A bag of marbles has 8 marbles. If I buy 2 bags of marbles, how many more bags of marbles would I need to buy to have a total of at least 45 marbles?

    A) 3
    B) 4
    C) 5
    D) 6
    E) 29

9) A factory that produces widgets wants to sell them each for $550. It costs $50 for the raw materials for each widget and the startup cost for the factory was $10000. How many widgets have to be sold so that the factory can break even?

    A) 10
    B) 20
    C) 30
    D) 40
    E) 50

10) Expand (3x-4)(6-2x).

   A) $6x^2-6x+8$
   B) $-6x^2+26x-24$
   C) $6x^2-26x+24$
   D) $-6x^2+26x+24$
   E) $6x^2+26x-24$

11) If 6n+m is divisible by 3 and 5, which of the following numbers when added to 6n+m will still give a result that is divisible by 3 and 5?

   A) 4
   B) 6
   C) 12
   D) 20
   E) 60

12) If x is negative and $x^3/5$ and $x/5$ both give the same result, what could be the value of x?

   A) -5
   B) -4
   C) 3
   D) 0
   E) -1

13) If m = 3548 and n = 235, then what is the value of m * n?

   A) 87940
   B) 843499
   C) 87900
   D) 8830
   E) 833780

14) A ball is thrown at a speed of 30mph. How far will it travel in 2 minutes and 35 seconds?

   A) 1.5 miles
   B) 1.20 miles
   C) 1.29 miles
   D) 1.3 miles
   E) 1.1 miles

15) Simplify $30(\sqrt{40} - \sqrt{60})$.

    A) $30(\sqrt{5} - \sqrt{15})$
    B) $30(\sqrt{10} + \sqrt{15})$
    C) $60(\sqrt{5} + \sqrt{15})$
    D) $60(\sqrt{10} - \sqrt{15})$
    E) 60

16) Simplify $30/(\sqrt{40} - \sqrt{60})$

    A) $3(\sqrt{5} + \sqrt{15})$
    B) $-3(\sqrt{5} - \sqrt{15})$
    C) $-3(\sqrt{10} + \sqrt{15})$
    D) $3(\sqrt{10} + \sqrt{15})$
    E) $3(\sqrt{10} - \sqrt{15})$

17) What is the least common multiple of 2, 3, 4, 5?

    A) 30
    B) 60
    C) 120
    D) 40
    E) 50

18) It costs \$6 to make a pen that sells for \$12. How many pens need to be sold to make a profit of \$60?

    A) 10
    B) 6
    C) 72
    D) 30
    E) 12

#1 Solution
Answer: D
If the number is divisible by 2, d should be even, and if the number is divisible by 5, then b has to equal 0.
Start by making both variables 0 and dividing by largest factor 7; 56800/7 = 8114.
Subtract 2 from 56800 = 56798 a number divisible by 2 and 7.
Next add a multiple of 7 that turns the last number to a 0; 6*7 = 42 and add to 56798.
56798 + 42 = 56840 divisible by 2, 5 and 7.
Skill: Algebra

#2 Solution
Answer: C
Carla's age is c, Megan's age is m; c = 3m; c-8 = m-8+18.
Solving, we substitute 3m for c in equation 2→3m-8 = m+10→m=9.
Skill: Algebraic Equations

#3 Solution
Answer: E
We know $(x^2-25) = (x+5)(x-5)$.
So $(x^2-25)/(x+5) = x-5$. At x = 0, f(0)=-5.
Skill: Algebraic Equations

#4 Solution
Answer: B
Let j be John's age and s be Sally's age.
j+4 = 2(s+4)
s-8 = 10→s = 18
So j+4 = 2(18+4)→j = 40.
Skill: Algebraic Equations

#5 Solution
Answer: A
If x is the number of marbles initially, then .25x goes to Vic, .2x goes to Robbie, and .1x goes to Jules.
The number left = x = (1-.25-.2-.1)=.45x.
Of that I give 6/20 to my brother =6/20*.45x.
I am left with .45x(1-(6/20)) = .315x.
We are also told .315x = 315→x = 1000.
Skill: Algebraic Equations

#6 Solution

Answer: C

Always read the question carefully! Questions 5 & 6 are similar, but they are not the same. Let x be the original number of marbles. After Vic's share is given .75x remains. After Robbie's share .75x*.80 remains. After Jules share .75x*.8*.9 remains, and after I give my brother his share .75x*.8*.9*(1-6/20) remains. The remaining number = .378x. We are told .378x = 315$\rightarrow$x = 833.33. We need to increase this to the next highest number, 834, because we have part of a marble and to include it we need to have a whole marble.

Skill: Algebraic Equations

#7 Solution

Answer: C

Replace the value of x with its value and solve the equation.

29 = 5y+4

Solving:

29-4 = 5y+4-4

25 = 5y or 5y = 25

5y/5 = 25/5

y = 5

Skill: Algebraic Equations

#8 Solution

Answer: B

2(8) + x > 45$\rightarrow$x > 29. We need more than 29 marbles. A bag has 8 marbles, so the number of bags needed is 29/8, which is 4. Since we need 3 bags + part of another bag, we need 4 additional bags to give at least 45 marbles.

Skill: Algebraic Equations

#9 Solution

Answer: B

The cost the factory incurs for making n widgets is 10000+50n; n is the number of widgets. The amount the factory makes by selling n widgets is 550n.

At the break-even point, the cost incurred is equal to the amount of sales.

10000+50n = 550n$\rightarrow$ n = 20.

Skill: Algebraic Equations

#10 Solution

Answer: B

Use FOIL: (3x-4)(6-2x) = 3x*6 -4*6 +3x*(-2x) -4*(-2x) = 18x-24-6x^2+8x = -6x^2+26x-24.

Skill: Algebraic Equations

#11 Solution

Answer: E

Since 6n+m is divisible by 3 and 5, the new number that we get after adding a value will be divisible by 3 and 5 only if the value that we add is divisible by 3 and 5. From the given choices, the only number that will work is 60.

Skill: Algebra

#12 Solution

Answer: E

We are told $x^3/5 = x/5 \rightarrow x^3 = x$. The possible values are -1, 0, 1. But we are told that x is negative. So x = -1.

Skill: Algebra

#13 Solution

Answer: E

This problem can be done by elimination. We know that m is in the thousands which means $x * 10^3$ and n is in the hundreds which is $y*10^2$. The answer will be $z * 10^5$ or 6 places in total, so we can eliminate A, C, and D. Also we see that m ends in 8 and n ends in 5, so the answer has to end in 0 (8*5 = 40), so we can eliminate B.

Skill: Algebra

#14 Solution

Answer: C

The ball has a speed of 30 miles per hour = 30 miles per 60 minutes = .5 mile per minute. 2 minutes and 35 seconds = 2 minutes and 35/60 minutes = 2.58 minutes. The ball travels .5 * 2.58 = 1.29 miles.

Skill: Algebra

#15 Solution

Answer: D

$30(\sqrt{40} - \sqrt{60}) = 60(\sqrt{10} - \sqrt{15})$

Skill: Algebra

#16 Solution

Answer: C

Multiply the numerator and denominator by $(\sqrt{40} + \sqrt{60})$.

So $30/(\sqrt{40} - \sqrt{60}) * [(\sqrt{40} + \sqrt{60})/(\sqrt{40} + \sqrt{60})] = 30(\sqrt{40} + \sqrt{60})/(\sqrt{40} - \sqrt{60})^2$
$= -3(\sqrt{10} + \sqrt{15})$.

Skill: Algebra

#17 Solution

Answer: B

Find all the prime numbers that multiply to give the numbers.

So for 2, prime factor 2; for 3, prime factor 3; for 4, prime factors 2, 2; for 5, prime factor 5. Note the maximum times of occurrence of each prime and multiply these to find the least common multiple. The LCM is 2*2*3*5 = 60.

Skill: Algebra

#18 Solution

Answer: A

One pen sells for $12, so on the sale of a pen, the profit is 12-6 = 6.

In order to make $60, we need to sell 10 pens.

Skill: Algebra

Section 5: Inequalities, Literal Equations, Linear Systems, Polynomials, Binomials

1) If x<5 and y<6, then x+y __ 11?

   A) <
   B) >
   C) ≤
   D) ≥
   E) =

2) Which of the following statements is true about the inequality $25x^2-40x-32 < 22$?

   A) There are no solutions
   B) There is a set of solutions
   C) There is 1 solution only
   D) There are 2 solutions
   E) There are 3 solutions

3) If x -2y > 6, what are possible values of y so x is always greater than or equal to 2?

   A) y≥1
   B) y≤0
   C) y≥-2
   D) y<2
   E) y≤6

4) Find the point of intersection of the lines x+2y = 4, 3x-y = 26.

   A) (1,3)
   B) (8,-2)
   C) (0,2)
   D) (2,-1)
   E) (4,26)

5) If a+b = 2 and a-b = 4, what is a?

    A) 1
    B) 2
    C) 3
    D) 4
    E) 5

6) If $\sqrt{a} + \sqrt{b} = 2$ and $\sqrt{a} - \sqrt{b} = 3$, what is a+b?

    A) 6.5
    B) 6
    C) 5.5
    D) 5
    E) 4.5

7) If a = b+3 and 3b = 5a+6, what is 3a-2b?

    A) -1.5
    B) 2.5
    C) 3
    D) 4.3
    E) 5

8) The sum of the roots of a quadratic equation is 8 and the difference is 2. What is the equation?

    A) $x^2-8x-15$
    B) $x^2+8x+15$
    C) $x^2-8x+15$
    D) $x^2+8x-15$
    E) x^2+15

9) Solve the following system of equations:
        3x+2y = 7 and 3x+y = 5.

    A) x = 2, y = 1
    B) x = 2, y = 2
    C) x = 1, y = 0
    D) x = 1, y = 2
    E) x = 1, y = 1

10) Nine tickets were sold for $41. If the tickets cost $4 and $5, how many $5 tickets were sold?

A) 5
B) 4
C) 9
D) 6
E) 7

11) Joe brought a bag of 140 M&Ms to his class that had 40 students. The boys each received two M&Ms and the girls each received four. How many boys were there in the class?

A) 10
B) 20
C) 30
D) 40
E) 50

<u>#1 Solution</u>
Answer: A
Choice A will always be true, while the other choices can never be true.
Skill: Inequalities

<u>#2 Solution</u>
Answer: B
$25x^2-40x+32<22 \rightarrow 25x^2-40x+16<6 \rightarrow (5x-4)^2<6 \rightarrow 5x-4<6$
x has to be all numbers less than 2 for this inequality to work, since x = 2.
Skill: Inequalities

<u>#3 Solution</u>
Answer: C
Rearrange equation: x > 6 + 2y, so 2 > 6 + 2y. Solve for y.
$2 \geq 6 + 2y$
$-4 \geq 2y$, so $-2 \leq y$ or $y \geq -2$
(When working with inequalities, remember to reverse the sign when dividing by a negative number).
Skill: Inequalities

<u>#4 Solution</u>
Answer: B
Find the slopes first. The slopes are -1/2 and 3. If they are not equal then the lines intersect.
Next, solve by substitution or addition. From the first equation, x = 4-2y. Plugging this into equation 2, we get $3(4-2y)-y = 26 \rightarrow 7y = 12-26 \rightarrow y = -2$. Plug this value into either equation to find x. If we plug into equation 1, we get $x-4 = 4 \rightarrow x = 8$.
Skill: Linear Systems

<u>#5 Solution</u>
Answer: C
Add the equations to eliminate $b \rightarrow 2a = 6 \rightarrow a = 3$.
Skill: Linear Systems

<u>#6 Solution</u>
Answer: A
Square both equations.
Equation 1 becomes $a+2\sqrt{ab}+b = 4$ and equation 2 becomes $a-2\sqrt{ab}+b = 9$.
Add the equations $\rightarrow 2(a+b) = 13 \rightarrow a+b = 13/2$.
Skill: Linear Systems

#7 Solution

Answer: A

Solve by substitution. $3b = 5(b+3) + 6$ $\qquad$ $a = -10.5 + 3 = -7.5$

$\qquad\qquad\qquad\qquad$ $3b - 5b - 15 = 6$

$\qquad\qquad\qquad\qquad$ $-2b = 21$ $\quad$ $b = -10.5$ $\qquad$ $3(-7.5) - 2(-10.5) = -1.5$

Skill: Linear Systems

#8 Solution

Answer: C

If the roots are a and b, then $a+b = 8$ and $a-b = 2$.

Add the equations: $2a = 10 \rightarrow a = 5 \rightarrow b = 3$.

The factors are $(x-5)(x-3)$ and the equation is $x^2-8x+15$.

Skill: Linear Systems

#9 Solution

Answer: D

From the equation $3x+y = 5$, we get $y = 5-3x$. Substitute into the other equation: $3x+2(5-3x) = 7 \rightarrow 3x+10-6x = 7 \rightarrow x = 1$. Plugging this value into either of the equations, we get $y = 2$.

Skill: Linear Systems

#10 Solution

Answer: A

$4x+5y = 41$, $x+y = 9$; where x and y are the number of tickets sold.

From equation 2, $x = 9-y$, and from equation 1, $4(9-y)+5y = 41 \rightarrow 36+y = 41 \rightarrow y = 5$.

Skill: Linear Systems

#11 Solution

Answer: A

If b is the number of boys and g is the number of girls, then $b+g = 40$ and $2b+4g = 140$.

To do the problem use the substitution method. From equation 1, $g = 40-b$.

Plug this into equation 2, $2b+4(40-b) = 140 \rightarrow b = 10$.

Skill: Linear Systems

Section 6: Slope, Distance to Midpoint, Graphing, Linear Equations

1) What is the equation of the line that passes through (3,5) with intercept y = 8?

   A) $y = x+8$
   B) $y = x-8$
   C) $y = -x-8$
   D) $y = -x+8$
   E) $y = -x$

2) What is the value of y in the equation $(3x-4)^2 = 4y-15$, if x = 3?

   A) 10
   B) 2.5
   C) -10
   D) -2.5
   E) 5

3) If Jennifer gets three times as much allowance as Judy gets, and Judy gets $5/week, how much does Jennifer get every month?

   A) $15
   B) $20
   C) $30
   D) $45
   E) $60

4) What is the value of x if y = 8 in the equation $5x + 9y = 3x - 6y + 5$?

   A) 57.5
   B) 60
   C) -60
   D) -57.5
   E) None of the above

5) What is the area outside the circle, but within the square, whose two corners are A and B?

A(3,5)   B (8,17)

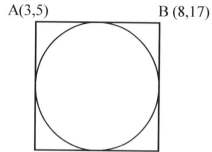

A) 169(1-π)
B) 169 π
C) 169 π /4
D) 169(1- π /4)
E) 169

6) Determine where the following two lines intersect:

$$3x + 4y = 7$$
$$9x + 12y = 21$$

A) x = 4, y = 3
B) x = 12, y = 9
C) x = 1/3, y = 1/3
D) Not enough information provided
E) There is no solution; the lines do not intersect

7) A line with a slope of 2 passes through the point (2,4). What is the set of coordinates when that line passes through the y intercept?

A) (-2,0)
B) (0,0)
C) (2,2)
D) (4,0)
E) (1,1)

8) Are the following lines parallel or perpendicular?

$$3x+4y = 7$$
$$8x-6y = 9$$

A) Parallel
B) Perpendicular
C) Neither parallel nor perpendicular
D) Cannot be determined
E) The angle at the point of intersection is 40

9) Two points on a line have coordinates (3,12) and (9,20). What is the distance between these two points?

A) 10
B) 12
C) 13
D) 8
E) 11

10) In the following graph, what is the equation of line AB if line AB is perpendicular to line PQ? Point coordinates are:
   M (-4,0), O (0,2), N (0,-3) and the lines intersect at (-2,1).

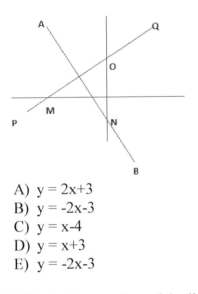

A) y = 2x+3
B) y = -2x-3
C) y = x-4
D) y = x+3
E) y = -2x-3

11) What is the equation of the line that passes through (1,2) and (6,12)?

A) y = x
B) y = 2x
C) y = x/2
D) y = 2x+2
E) y = x-2

12) What is the midpoint of the line connecting points (0,8) and (2,6)?

A) (-1,1)
B) (2,14)
C) (-2,2)
D) (0,1)
E) (1,7)

13) What is the equation of the line passing through (1,1) and (2,4)?

    A) $3y = x + 2$
    B) $2y = x + 3$
    C) $y = 3x - 2$
    D) $4x = y + 2$
    E) $y = (1/3)x + 2$

14) Line A passes through (0,0) and (3,4). Line B passes through (2,6) and (3,y). What value of y will make the lines parallel?

    A) 20/3
    B) 7
    C) 22/3
    D) 29
    E) 5

15) Line A passes through (1,3) and (3,4). Line B passes through (3,7) and (5,y). What value of y will make the lines perpendicular?

    A) 1
    B) 2
    C) 3
    D) 4
    E) 5

16) What is the equation of line A that is perpendicular to line B, connecting (8,1) and (10,5), that intersects at (x,14)?

    A) $y = 2x - 7$
    B) $y = -2x + 7$
    C) $y = (-1/2)x + 19\frac{1}{4}$
    D) $y = 5x - 7$
    E) $y = 2x - 19\frac{1}{4}$

#1 Solution
Answer: D
The standard form of the line equation is $y = mx+b$.
We need to find slope m, $m = (y_2-y_1)/(x_2-x_1)$ ➔ $m = (5-8)/(3-0)$ ➔ $m = -1$.
Therefore the equation is $y = -x+8$.
Skill: Linear Equations

#2 Solution
Answer: A
At $x = 3$, $((3\cdot3) - 4)^2 = 4y - 15$
$\qquad (9 - 4)^2 = 4y - 15$
$\qquad\quad 25 = 4y - 15$
$\qquad\quad 40 = 4y \qquad y = 10$
Skill: Literal Equations

#3 Solution
Answer: E
If Judy gets x dollars, then Jennifer gets 3x in a week. In a month, Jennifer will then get 4*3x.
If Judy gets $5 per week, then Jennifer gets $60 in a month.
Skill: Literal equation

#4 Solution
Answer: D
Combine like terms.
$5x+9y = 3x-6y+5$ ➔ $2x = -15y+5$ ➔ $x = -57.5$ when $y = 8$.
Skill: Literal equations

#5 Solution
Answer: D
First we need to find the length of side AB: $AB = \sqrt{(17-5)^2+(8-3)^2} = 13$.
If $AB = 13$, then $A_{square} = 13^2 = 169$.
AB is also the diameter of the circle. $A_{circle} \pi (d^2/4) = 169 \pi /4$.
The area outside the circle and within the square is:
$A_{square}-A_{circle} = 169(1- \pi /4)$.
Skill: Geometry & Slope, Distance, Graphing

#6 Solution
Answer: E
While it is tempting to solve this system of simultaneous equations to find the values of x and y, the first thing to do is to see whether the lines intersect. To do this, compare the slopes of the two lines by putting the lines into the standard form $y = mx+b$, where m is the slope.
By rearranging, equation 1 becomes $y = 7/4-3x/4$ and equation 2 becomes $y = 21/12-9x/12$.

The slope of line 1 is -3/4 and the slope of line 2 is -9/12, which is -3/4 when reduced. Since the slopes are equal, the lines are parallel and do not intersect.
Skill: Slope, Distance to Midpoint, Graphing

#7 Solution
Answer: B
The slope of the line is given as $m = (y_2-y_1)/(x_2-x_1)$ where (x_1,y_1) and (x_2,y_2) are two points the line passes through. The y intercept is the point where the graph intersects the y axis, so x = 0 at this point.
Plugging in the values of m, etc., we get $2 = (4-y)/(2-0) \rightarrow y = 0$.
Skill: Slope, Distance to Midpoint, Graphing

#8 Solution
Answer: B
Find the slopes by rearranging the two equations into the form y = mx+b.
Equation 1 becomes y = -3x/4+7/4 and equation 2 becomes y = 8x/6-9/6.
So $m_1 = -3/4$ and $m_2 = 8/6 = 4/3$. We see that m_1 is the negative inverse of m_2, so line 1 is perpendicular to line 2.
Skill: Slope, Distance to Midpoint, Graphing

#9 Solution
Answer: A
Distance $s = \sqrt{(x_2-x_1)^2+(y_2-y_1)^2} \rightarrow s = \sqrt{(9-3)^2+(20-12)^2} = \sqrt{36+64} = 10$.
Skill: Slope, Distance to Midpoint, Graphing

#10 Solution
Answer: B
y = mx + b; m is the slope and b is the y intercept. Calculate m for line AB using the given points (0,-3) and (-2, 1). m = (-3 -1)/(0-(-2)) = -2. The y intercept is -3 (from point set given), so y = -2x-3.
Skill: Slope, Distance to Midpoint, Graphing

#11 Solution
Answer: B
First find the slope, $(y_2-y_1)/(x_2-x_1) \rightarrow$ slope = (12-2)/(6-1) = 2.
Next, use the slope and a point to find the value of b.
In the standard line equation, y = mx+b, use the point (6,12) to get
12 = (2*6)+b→b = 0.
The equation of the line is y = 2x.
Skill: Slope, Distance to Midpoint, Graphing

#12 Solution
Answer: E
The midpoint is at $(x_1+x_2)/2, (y_1+y_2)/2 = (1,7)$.
Skill: Slope, Distance to Midpoint, Graphing

#13 Solution
Answer: C
Slope = $(y_2-y_1)/(x_2-x_1) = 3$. Plug one of the coordinates into $y = mx+b$ to find the value of b.
$1 = 3(1)+b \rightarrow b = -2$.
The equation of the line is $y = 3x - 2$.
Skill: Slope, Distance to Midpoint, Graphing

#14 Solution
Answer: C
Start by calculating the slope of each line. Slope of line A = 4/3 and slope of line B = y-6.
The slopes of the line have to be the same for the lines to be parallel.
$\rightarrow 4/3 = y-6 \rightarrow 4 = 3y-18 \rightarrow y = 22/3$.
Skill: Slope, Distance to Midpoint, Graphing

#15 Solution
Answer: C
The slope of line A = 1/2 and the slope of line B = (y-7)/2.
The product of the slopes has to equal -1.
$\rightarrow (1/2)[(y-7)/2] = -1 \rightarrow (y-7)/4 = -1 \rightarrow y = 3$
Skill: Slope, Distance to Midpoint, Graphing

#16 Solution
Answer: C
Slope$_b$ = $(5-1)/(10-8) = 2$. The slope of line A is -1/2.
To find the intercept of line B, use $y = mx+b$: $5 = (2)(10)+b$, so $b = -7$. Equation of line B is $y = 2x - 7$.
Find the intersect x using the given y coordinate; $14 = 2x - 7$; $x = 10.5$.
Find the intercept of line A using the coordinates of intersection: $14 = (-1/2)(10.5)+b$; $b = 19\frac{1}{4}$.
The equation of line A is $y = -(1/2)x+19\frac{1}{4}$.
Skill: Geometry & Slope

Section 7: Quadratics, Functions, Absolute Value Equations,

1) Factor $x^2+2x-15$.

  A) $(x-3)(x+5)$
  B) $(x+3)(x-5)$
  C) $(x+3)(x+5)$
  D) $(x-3)(x-5)$
  E) $(x-1)(x+15)$

2) Car A starts at 3:15 p.m. and travels straight to its destination at a constant speed of 50 mph. If it arrives at 4:45 p.m., how far did it travel?

  A) 70 miles
  B) 75 miles
  C) 65 miles
  D) 40 miles
  E) 105 miles

3) What are the roots of the equation $2x^2+14x = 0$?

  A) 0 and 7
  B) 0 and -7
  C) 14 and 0
  D) 2 and 14
  E) Cannot be determined

4) If $f(x) = 2x^2+3x$, and $g(x) = x+4$, what is $f[g(x)]$?

  A) $x^2+19x+44$
  B) $2x^2+19x+44$
  C) $4x^2+35x+76$
  D) $x^2+8x+16$
  E) None of the above

5) If $|x+4| = 2$, what are the values of x?

  A) 2 and 6
  B) -2 and -6
  C) -2
  D) -6
  E) 0

6) The sales of an item can be written as a function of price: $s = 3p+c$, where s is the amount in sales, p is the price charged per item, and c is a constant value. If the sales generated are $20 at a price of $5 for the item, then what should the price be to generate $50 in sales?

    A) $10
    B) $15
    C) $20
    D) $16
    E) $14

7) If $f(n) = 2n + 3\sqrt{n}$, where n is a positive integer, what is $f[g(5)]$ if $g(m) = m-4$?

    A) 1
    B) 2
    C) 3
    D) 4
    E) 5

8) An equation has two roots: 5 and -8. What is a possible equation?

    A) $x^2-3x+40$
    B) $x^2-3x-40$
    C) x^2+x+40
    D) $x^2+3x-40$
    E) $2x^2-3x+40$

9) The sum of the roots of a quadratic equation is 13 and the product is 36. What is the equation?

    A) $x^2+13x+36$
    B) $x^2-13x+36$
    C) $x^2-13x-36$
    D) $x^2+13x-36$
    E) $x^2+14x+36$

10) In an ant farm, the number of ants grows every week according to the formula: $N = 100+2^w$, where w is the number of weeks elapsed. How many ants will the colony have after 5 weeks?

    A) 115
    B) 125
    C) 135
    D) 132
    E) 233

11) If $|x| = 4$ and $|y| = 5$, what are the values of $|x+y|$?

    A) 1,9
    B) -1,9
    C) -1,-9
    D) -1,-9
    E) $1<|x+y|<9$

12) If $y = |x|$, what is the range of y?

    A) y<0
    B) 0<y<x
    C) y>0
    D) y≥0
    E) y>x

<u>#1 Solution</u>
Answer: A
The constant term is -15. The factors should multiply to give -15 and add to give 2.
The numbers -3 and 5 satisfy both, (x-3)(x+5).
Skill: Quadratics

<u>#2 Solution</u>
Answer: B.
The time between 3:15 pm and 4:45pm = 1.5 hrs.
1.5 * 50 = 75
Reminder: half an hour is written as .5 of an hour, not .3 of an hour, even though on a clock a half hour is 30 minutes.
Skill: Functions

<u>#3 Solution</u>
Answer: B
Rearrange, reduce, and factor.

$$2x^2 + 14x + 0 = 0$$
$$2(x^2 + 7x + 0) = 0$$
$$(x + 7)(x + 0)$$
$$x = 0 \quad \text{or} \quad -7$$

Skill: Quadratic Equations

<u>#4 Solution</u>
Answer: B
Substitute g(x) for every x in f(x).
$f[g((x+4))] = 2(x+4)^2 + 3(x+4) = 2x^2 + 16x + 32 + 3x + 12 = 2x^2 + 19x + 44$
Skill: Functions

<u>#5 Solution</u>
Answer: B
Two solutions: (x+4) = 2 and –(x+4) = 2.
Or x+4 = 2, x = -2.
And x+4 = -2, x = -6.
Skill: Absolute Value Equations

<u>#6 Solution</u>
Answer: B
Find the value of the constant by plugging in the given information.
20 = 3*5+c→c = 5.
Now use the value of c and the new value of s to find p→50 = 3p+5→p = 15.
Skill: Functions

#7 Solution

Answer: E

$g(5) = 5-4 = 1$. $f[g(5)] = 2*1+3\sqrt{1} = 5$.

Skill: Functions

#8 Solution

Answer: D

If the roots are 5 and -8, the factors are (x-5)(x+8). Multiply the factors to get the equation.

$x^2+3x-40$

Skill: Quadratic Equations

#9 Solution

Answer: B

If the sum is 13 and the product is 36, the roots are 4, 9. The factors are (x-4) and (x-9).

The equation is $x^2-13x+36$.

Skills: Quadratic Equations

#10 Solution

Answer: D

After 5 weeks the number of ants = 100+32 = 132.

Skill: Function

#11 Solution

Answer: A

$x = 4$ and $y = 5$, $|x+y| = 9$

$x = -4$ and $y = 5$, $|x+y| = 1$

$x = 4$ and $y = -5$, $|x+y| = 1$

$x = -4$ and $y = -5$, $|x+y| = 9$

Skill: Absolute Value Equations

#12 Solution

Answer: D

The absolute value of x can be at the least a 0, and is otherwise positive regardless of the value of x.

$y \geq 0$

Skill: Absolute Value

Section 8: Geometry

1) What is the area outside the circle, but within the square, whose two corners are A and B?

A(3,5)   B (8,17)

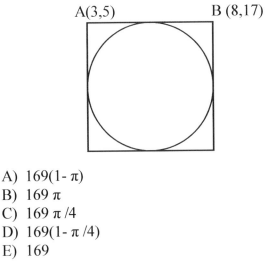

   A) 169(1- π)
   B) 169 π
   C) 169 π /4
   D) 169(1- π /4)
   E) 169

2) What is the area, in square feet, of the triangle whose sides have lengths equal to 3, 4, and 5 feet?

   A) 6 square feet
   B) 7 square feet
   C) 4 square feet
   D) 5 square feet
   E) 8 square feet

3) In the following figure, where AE bisects line BC, and angles AEC and AEB are both right angles, what is the length of AB?

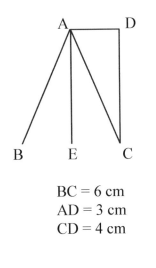

   BC = 6 cm
   AD = 3 cm
   CD = 4 cm

A) 1 cm
B) 2 cm
C) 3 cm
D) 4 cm
E) 5 cm

4) In the following triangle, if AB = 6 and BC = 8, what should the length of CA be to make triangle ABC a right triangle?

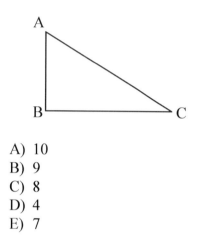

A) 10
B) 9
C) 8
D) 4
E) 7

5) In the following circle there is a square with an area of 36 cm^2. What is the area outside the square, but within the circle?

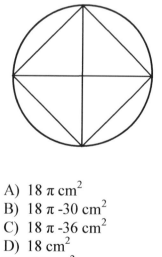

A) 18 π cm^2
B) 18 π -30 cm^2
C) 18 π -36 cm^2
D) 18 cm^2
E) -18 cm^2

6) If a square of area 25 cm² is rotated around the side AB, what is the volume of the resulting shape?

    A) 625
    B) 625 π
    C) 125 π
    D) 25 π^2
    E) 625 π^2

7) The length of a rectangle is 4 times its width. If the width of the rectangle is 5-x inches and the perimeter of the rectangle is 30 in, what is x?

    A) 1
    B) 2
    C) 3
    D) 4
    E) 5

8) If in triangle ABC, AB/AC = 6/10, then what is BC/AB?

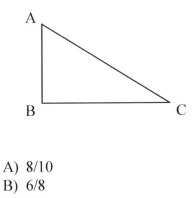

    A) 8/10
    B) 6/8
    C) 4/5
    D) 2/5
    E) 5/8

9) Two sides of a triangle have a ratio AC/BC = 5/4. The length of AB on a similar triangle = 24. What is the actual value of AC for the larger triangle?

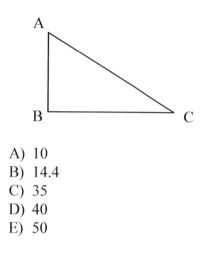

A) 10
B) 14.4
C) 35
D) 40
E) 50

10) If the diameter of a circle is doubled, the area increases by what factor?

A) 1 time
B) 2 times
C) 3 times
D) 4 times
E) 5 times

11) A rectangular prism has length = 4cm, width = 5cm, and height = 10cm. It weighs 6 kg. If the length is cut in half, the width is doubled, and the height stays the same, how much will the resulting rectangular prism weigh?

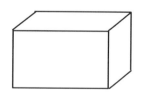

A) 6 kg
B) 3 kg
C) 200 g
D) 400 g
E) 5 kg

12) In the following figure, what is A?

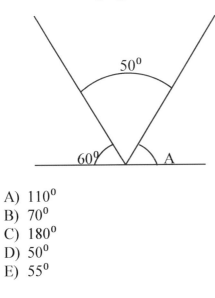

A) 110^0
B) 70^0
C) 180^0
D) 50^0
E) 55^0

13) In the following isosceles triangle, what is the largest possible value of angle B?

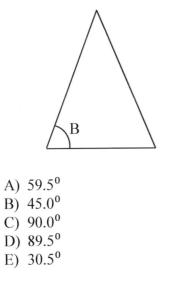

A) 59.5^0
B) 45.0^0
C) 90.0^0
D) 89.5^0
E) 30.5^0

14) In the following figure, what are the values of angles A, B and C?

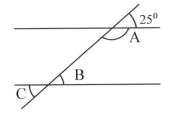

A) $\angle A = 155^0$, $\angle B = 25^0$, $\angle C = 25^0$
B) $\angle A = 145^0$, $\angle B = 20^0$, $\angle C = 20^0$
C) $\angle A = 150^0$, $\angle B = 25^0$, $\angle C = 25^0$
D) $\angle A = 55^0$, $\angle B = 35^0$, $\angle C = 45^0$
E) $\angle A = 155^0$, $\angle B = 35^0$, $\angle C = 25^0$

15) In the following triangle PQR, what is the measure of angle A?

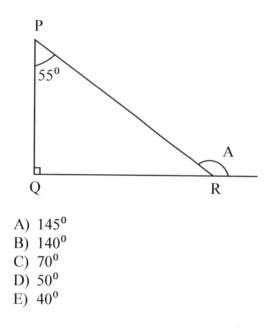

A) 145^0
B) 140^0
C) 70^0
D) 50^0
E) 40^0

16) In the triangle ABC, the length of AB = 5 and the length of BC = 7. Which of the following cannot be the length of AC?

A) 3
B) 6
C) 11
D) 12
E) 10

#1 Solution

Answer: D

First find the length of side AB: AB = $\sqrt{(17-5)2 + (8-3)2}$ = 13.

If AB = 13, then A_{square} = 132 = 169.

AB is also the diameter of the circle, so A $_{circle}$ π (d^2/4) = 169 π /4.

The area outside the circle, but within the square is:

A $_{square}$ – A $_{circle}$ = 169(1- π /4).

Skill: Geometry & Slope, Distance, Graphing

#2 Solution

Answer: A

The Pythagorean triple (special right triangle property) means the two shorter sides form a right triangle.

1/2bh = A

(1/2)(3)(4) = 6

Skill: Geometry

#3 Solution

Answer: E

AB^2 = AC^2 = AD2+CD^2 → AB^2 = 3^2+4^2 → AB = 5

Skill: Geometry

#4 Solution

Answer: A

In a right triangle, the square of the hypotenuse = the sum of the squares of the other two sides. AB^2+BC^2 = AC^2 → AC^2 = 36+64 → AC = 10.

Skill: Geometry

#5 Solution

Answer: C

If the area of the square is 36cm^2, then each side is 6cm. If we look at the triangle made by half the square, that diagonal would be the hypotenuse of the triangle, and its length = $\sqrt{6^2+6}$ ^{2} = 6√2.

This hypotenuse is also the diameter of the circle, so the radius of the circle is 3√2.

The area of the circle =$A = \pi r^2$= 18π.

The area outside the square, but within the circle is 18π -36.

Skill: Geometry

<u>#6 Solution</u>
Answer: C
If the area of the square is 25cm^2, then a side will be 5 cm. If the square is rotated around side AB, which is 5 cm, then the top of the square will sweep a circular area of radius 5 cm to form a three dimensional cylinder. Volume of a cylinder:
V = π *r^2*h = (5^2)*5* π = 125π.
Skill: Geometry

<u>#7 Solution</u>
Answer: B
Perimeter of a rectangle = 2(l+w).
Width = 5-x and length = 4(5-x).
Perimeter = 2(l*w) = 30→2(20-4x+5-x) = 30→-10x = -20→x = 2.
Skill: Geometry

<u>#8 Solution</u>
Answer: A
If the ratio of AB:AC = 6:10, regardless of what the actual value of AB or AC is, this ratio is always constant.
Assuming that AB = 6 and AC = 8, BC = $\sqrt{(AC2 - AB2)}$ = 8.
BC/AB = 8/10, which is still a ratio, so it does not matter what the actual values are.
Skill: Geometry

<u>#9 Solution</u>
Answer: D
Side AC = 5 and side BC = 4. The Pythagorean triple is 3:4:5, so side AB = 3.
Because the other triangle is similar, the ratio of all sides is constant. AB:AB = 3:24.
The ratio factor is 8. AC of the larger triangle = 5 * 8 = 40.
Skill: Geometry

<u>#10 Solution</u>
Answer: D
The area of a circle = π * r^2.
If the diameter is doubled, then the radius is also doubled.
The new area = π*(2r)^2 = 4 *π *r^2. The area increases four times.
Skill: Geometry

<u>#11 Solution</u>
Answer: A
Original volume$_{4,5,10}$ = 4*5*10 = 200 cm^3.
New volume$_{2,10,10}$ = 2*10*10 = 200 cm^3.
If 1 cm^3 is 30gm, then 200cm^3 will be 6000gm = 6 kg.
Skill: Geometry

#12 Solution
Answer: B
The angle of a straight line $= 180^0$.
$60^0+50^0+\angle A = 180^0 \rightarrow \angle A = 70^0$.
Skill: Geometry

#13 Solution
Answer: D
The sum of the three angles of a triangle $= 180^0$. According to the definition of an isosceles triangle, the two angles that are opposite the two equal sides are also equal. The third angle has to be at least 1^0. The sum of the other two angles $= 180-1$ or 179^0. Half of $179^0 = 89.5^0$.
Skill: Geometry

#14 Solution
Answer: A
$\angle A + 25^0 = 180^0$; $\angle A = 155^0$ (Supplementary Angles).
$\angle B = 25^0$ (Corresponding Angles).
$\angle B = \angle C$; $\angle C = 25^0$ (Opposite Angles).
Skill: Geometry

#15 Solution
Answer: A
$\angle P = 55^0$; $\angle Q = 90^0$. $\angle R = 180-(55+90) = 35^0$ and $\angle A = 180-35 = 145^0$.
Skill: Geometry

#16 Solution
Answer: D
In any triangle, the sum of two sides of the triangle has to be greater than the length of the third side. The sum of the given sides $= 12$. The third side has to be less than 12.
Skill: Geometry

Section 9: Fundamental Counting Principle

1) The wardrobe of a studio contains four hats, three suits, five shirts, two pants, and three pairs of shoes. How many different ways can these items be put together?

   A) 60
   B) 300
   C) 360
   D) 420
   E) 500

2) For lunch you have a choice between chicken fingers or cheese sticks for an appetizer, turkey, chicken, or veal for the main course, cake or pudding for dessert, and either Coke or Pepsi for a beverage. How many choices of possible meals do you have?

   A) 16
   B) 24
   C) 34
   D) 36
   E) 8

3) At a buffet, there are 3 choices for an appetizer, 6 choices for a beverage, and 3 choices for an entrée. How many different ways can I select food from all the food choices?

   A) 12
   B) 27
   C) 36
   D) 42
   E) 54

<u>#1 Solution</u>
Answer: C
The number of ways = 4*3*5*2*3 = 360.
Skill: Fundamental Counting Principle

<u>#2 Solution</u>
Answer: B
Multiply the possible number of choices for each item from which you can choose:
2 * 3 * 2 * 2 = 24.
Skill: Fundamental Counting Principle

<u>#3 Solution</u>
Answer: E
There are 3 ways to choose an appetizer, 6 ways to choose a beverage, and 3 ways to choose an entrée. The total number of choices = 3*6*3 = 54.
Skill: Fundamental Counting Principle

Section 10: Probabilities, Ratios, Proportions, Rate of Change

1) A class has 50% more boys than girls. What is the ratio of boys to girls?

    A) 4:3
    B) 3:2
    C) 5:4
    D) 10:7
    E) 7:5

2) A car can travel 30 miles on 4 gallons of gas. If the gas tank has a capacity of 16 gallons, how far can it travel if the tank is ¾ full?

    A) 120 miles
    B) 90 miles
    C) 60 miles
    D) 55 miles
    E) 65 miles

3) The profits of a company increase by $5000 every year for five years and then decrease by $2000 for the next two years. What is the average rate of change in the company profit for that seven-year period?

    A) $1000/yr
    B) $2000/yr
    C) $3000/yr
    D) $4000/yr
    E) $5000/yr

4) A bag holds 250 marbles. Of those marbles, 40% are red, 30% are blue, 10% are green, and 20% are black. How many marbles of each color are present in the bag?

    A) Red = 90, blue = 80, green = 30, black = 40
    B) Red = 80, blue = 60, green = 30, black = 80
    C) Red = 100, blue = 75, green = 25, black = 50
    D) Red = 100, blue = 70, green = 30, black = 50
    E) Red = 120, blue = 100, green = 10, black = 20

5) Two students will be selected to serve on the school disciplinary committee from a student body of 30 boys and 50 girls. What is the probability that first a boy will chosen, then a girl?

   A) 1/1500
   B) 1500/6400
   C) 1500/6320
   D) 1
   E) 30/50

6) If a number n, divided by a number m, gives a result of .5, what is the relationship between n and m?

   A) n is twice as big as m
   B) m is three times as big as n
   C) n is a negative number
   D) m is a negative number
   E) n is ½ of m

7) In a fruit basket, there are 10 apples, 5 oranges, 5 pears, and 6 figs. If I select two fruits, what is the probability that I will pick a pear first and then an apple?

   A) .07
   B) .08
   C) 1/13
   D) 13
   E) 5

8) In a fruit basket, there are 3 apples, 5 oranges, 2 pears, and 2 figs. If I pick out two fruits, what is the probability that I will pick a fig first and then an apple?
Round to the nearest 100th.

   A) .04
   B) .05
   C) .06
   D) .03
   E) .02

9) If x workers can make p toys in c days, how many toys can y workers make in d days if they work at the same rate?

A) cp/qx
B) cq/px
C) cqy/px
D) pdy/cx
E) qy/px

10) If a car travels 35 miles on a gallon of gas, how far will it travel on 13 gallons of gas?

A) 189 miles
B) 255 miles
C) 335 miles
D) 455 miles
E) 500 miles

11) If x workers can do a job in y days, how long will it take x+5 workers to do the same job?

A) $(x+5)y$
B) $(x+5)y^2$
C) $(x^2-5)/y$
D) $(x^2+5x)/y$
E) (x^2+5)

12) If 20% of c is equal to 40% of d, what is c/d?

A) 1
B) 2
C) 3
D) 4
E) 5

13) A dealer increased the price of a car by 30%, but then discounted it by 30%. What is the relationship between the final price and the original price?

A) .91x : x
B) .98x : x
C) 1 : 1
D) .88x : x
E) .75x : x

14) If 3/5 of a class of 20 students are girls, what is the ratio of boys: girls?

    A) 1/3
    B) 2
    C) 3
    D) 2/3
    E) 1

15) Andy can paint a wall in 3 hours. Mike can paint the same wall in 4 hours. How much time will it take them to paint the wall together?

    A) 1 hour and 16 minutes
    B) 2 hours
    C) 2 hours and 35 minutes
    D) 1 hour and 42 minutes
    E) Not enough information provided

16) A bank account has $35000. The money is split into 14 shares. John gets 2 shares, Mary gets 4 shares, Cindy gets 5 shares, and Jessica gets the rest. How much money does Jessica get?

    A) $10500
    B) $7500
    C) $8000
    D) $4500
    E) $5300

17) A 2400 acre plot of land is split into 5 parts. The first part is 30%, the second part is 5%, the third part is 20%, and the fourth part is 10%. On a pie chart, what angles do each of the divisions represent?

    A) $108°, 18°, 72°, 36°, 126°$
    B) $108°, 20°, 72°, 36°, 124°$
    C) $106°, 20°, 72°, 36°, 126°$
    D) $30°, 5°, 20°, 10°, 35°$
    E) $108°, 18°, 72°, 36°, 124°$

18) A bag of M&Ms has a total of 30 M&Ms. The bag contains 40% blue M&Ms, 20% red M&Ms, and 10% brown M&Ms. It also contains green M&Ms. What is the probability that two green M&Ms will be picked up in one handful?

   A) 81/900
   B) 81/870
   C) 81/290
   D) 24/290
   E) 12/150

19) Bag A holds 2 apples and 1 banana. Bag B holds 1 apple and 2 bananas. What is the probability of picking a banana from each bag?

   A) 1/3
   B) 2/3
   C) 1/9
   D) 2/9
   E) 2

20) Bag A holds 3 apples and 3 bananas. What is the probability of picking two bananas?

   A) 1/4
   B) 6/20
   C) .20
   D) 9/30
   E) 1/10

#1 Solution
Answer: B
The ratio of boys to girls is 150 : 100 or 3 : 2.
Skill: Ratios

#2 Solution
Answer: B
A full tank has 16 gallons→3/4 of the tank = 12 gallons. The car can travel 30 miles on 4 gallons, so 12 gallons would take the car 12*30/4 = 90 miles.
Skill: Proportions

#3 Solution
Answer: C
Average Rate of Change = the change in value/change in time = (total profit – initial profit)/change in time. Initial profit = 0, change in time = 7 yrs.
Increase = 5,000 x 5 = 25,000; decrease = 2,000 x 2 = 4,000; total profit = 25,000-4,000 = 21,000. (21,000-0)/ 7 yrs = $3,000/yr.
Skill: Rate of Change

#4 Solution
Answer: C
Total number of marbles = 250.
#red marbles = 250*40/100 = 250*.4 = 100.
#blue marbles = 250*.3 = 75.
#green marbles = 250*.1 = 25.
#black marbles = 250*.2 = 50.
Skill: Ratios

#5 Solution
Answer: C
The probability of selecting a boy from the entire group = 30/80.
The probability of selecting a girl from the remaining group = 50/79.
The probability of selecting a boy and a girl is (30/80)(50/79) = 1500/6320.
Skill: Probability

#6 Solution
Answer: E
If n/m = .5, then n = .5m or n = ½ of m.
Skill: Ratios

<u>#7 Solution</u>
Answer: C
The total number of fruit = 26.
The probability of picking a pear = 5/26.
The probability of picking an apple = 10/25.
The probability of picking a pear and an apple = 5/26 * 10/25 = 50/650 = 5/65 = 1/13.
Skill: Probability

<u>#8 Solution</u>
Answer: B
The total number of fruit = 12.
The probability of picking a fig = 2/12.
The probability of picking an apple = 3/11.
The probability of picking a fig and an apple = 2/12 * 3/11 = 6/132 = .045→round up to .05.
Skill: Probability

<u>#9 Solution</u>
Answer: C
The overall rate for x workers = the number of toys/divided by the number of days, *p/c*. The number of toys one worker makes per day (rate) = *p/cx*. If *q* is the number of toys *y* workers make, and the rates are equal, then the number of toys made = the rate x. The number of days x the number of workers; we have *q* = *p/cx* (*dy*) so
q = pdy/cx.
Skill: Ratios

<u>#10 Solution</u>
Answer: D
The distance travelled = (35/1)(13) = 455 miles.
Skill: Ratios

<u>#11 Solution</u>
Answer: D
It might be tempting to think of this as a direct ratio; if one increases, the other increases too. However, this is an inverse ratio; x+5 workers is greater than x workers so the time required would decrease.

The ratios are inverse→ y/x = x+5/n; where n is the number of days.
n = $(x^2+5x)/y$.
Skill: Ratios

#12 Solution

Answer: B

20% of c = 40% of d➔.2c = .4d➔c/d = 2.

Skill: Ratios

#13 Solution

Answer: A

Let the original price of the car be x.

After the 30% increase, the price is 1.3x.

After discounting the increased price by 30%, it is now .7*1.3x = .91x.

The ratio of the final price to the original price = .91x : x.

Skill: Percentages and Ratios

#14 Solution

Answer: D

If 3/5 of the class is girls, then 2/5 is boys.

The ratio of boys to girls = 2/3.

Skill: Ratios

#15 Solution

Answer: D.

If Andy paints 1 wall in 3 hours, he will only be able to paint 1/3 of the wall in 1 hour. If Mike paints 1 wall in 4 hours, he will only be able to paint 1/4 of the wall in 1 hour. If Mike and Andy work together to paint the wall for 1 hour, they will paint 1/3+1/4 of the wall or 7/12 of the wall.

If x is the total number of hours needed for them to finish painting the wall, then (7/12) * x = 1.

x = 12/7 = 1.71, round to 1.7.

1.7 hours = 1 hour + .7 hr = 1 hour + .7*60 minutes = 1 hour and 42 minutes.

Skill: Proportions

#16 Solution

Answer: B

Total number of shares = 14. Therefore Jessica's part is 14-(2+4+5) = 3.

So Jessica's share of the inheritance = 3/14*35000 = 7500.

Skill: Proportions

#17 Solution

Answer: A

The angle around the center of a circle = 360°.

The part that is 30% subtends an angle of 30/100 * 360 = 108°.

The part that is 5% subtends an angle of 5/100 * 360 = 18°.

The part that is 20% subtends an angle of 20/100 * 360 = 72°.

The part that is 10% subtends an angle of 10/100 * 360 = 36°.

The remaining part that is 35% subtends an angle of 35/100 * 360 = 126°.

Skill: Proportions

#18 Solution

Answer: D

First find the portion of each color.

Blue: .4*30 = 12.

Red: .2*30 = 6.

Brown: .1*30 = 3.

Green: 9.

The probability of picking two green M&Ms in one handful:

9/30 * 8/29 = 3/10 * 8/29 = 24/290.

Skill: Probability

#19 Solution

Answer: D

$Prob_{Bag\ A}$ = 1/3.

$Prob_{Bag\ B}$ = 2/3.

The total probability = (1/3)(2/3).

Skill: Probability

#20 Solution

Answer: C

$Prob_1$ = 3/6.

$Prob_2$ = 2/5.

The total probability = (3/6)(2/5) = 6/30 = 1/5 = .2.

Skill: Probability

Chapter 8: Critical Reading Question Bank

For the following questions, select the answer choice with the word or words that best fit in the sentence.

1. The investor seemed almost ------: she knew which stocks to select before they rose in value.
   a. circumspect
   b. prescient
   c. audacious
   d. discerning
   e. obtuse

2. The team of biologists was well prepared for the ------ climate in which they would be working; the tents and clothing they brought were all ------ to water.
   a. equatorial....impervious
   b. arid...impenetrable
   c. humid...porous
   d. parched...repulsive
   e. tempestuous...susceptible

3. Library cataloguing systems have always been important in ------ vast collections of knowledge; however, as information is increasingly ------, methods of organizing it are changing.
   a. organizing...diminished
   b. documenting...depleted
   c. confounding...uploaded
   d. systematizing...digitized
   e. collating...proliferated

4. Linda went to the meeting on the ------ of hearing about the new plan; in reality, she went because she wanted to spend some time away from her desk.
   a. hunch
   b. rationale
   c. pretext
   d. motive
   e. deception

5. If elected, the candidate's first priority would be to ------ the laws which were negatively affecting his constituency.
   a. allay
   b. sanction
   c. abrogate
   d. ratify
   e. lampoon

6. The chefs disagreed about the effect of an unusual spice in the dish: one felt that it added ------ to an otherwise standard meal, while the other maintained that it ------ the cuisine.
    a. pungency...ravaged
    b. relish...augmented
    c. redolence...buttressed
    d. drivel...rectified
    e. zest...undermined

7. It is important to think ------ when learning about a new place because the culture, the history, the geography, and the politics all interact to enable true understanding.
    a. discordantly
    b. discretely
    c. critically
    d. holistically
    e. authentically

8. Astronomers in the 15th century were not using the types of ------ instruments we have today; rather, they successfully ------ the distances between planetary bodies using observations and what they understood about physics on Earth.
    a. precise...deduced
    b. redundant...concluded
    c. meticulous...appraised
    d. efficacious...promulgated
    e. sophisticated...generalized

Questions 9 – 12 are based on the following passage:

From *"On Lying Awake at Night"* by Stewart Edward White (public domain)

About once in so often you are due to lie awake at night. Why this is so I have never been able to discover. It apparently comes from no predisposing uneasiness of indigestion, no rashness in the matter of too much tea or tobacco, no excitation of unusual incident or stimulating conversation. In fact, you turn in with the expectation of rather a good night's rest. Almost at once the little noises of the forest grow larger, blend in the hollow bigness of the first drowse; your thoughts drift idly back and forth between reality and dream; when—*snap!*—you are broad awake!

For, unlike mere insomnia, lying awake at night in the woods is pleasant. The eager, nervous straining for sleep gives way to a delicious indifference. You do not care. Your mind is cradled in an exquisite poppy-suspension of judgment and of thought. Impressions slip vaguely into your consciousness and as vaguely out again. Sometimes they stand stark and naked for your inspection; sometimes they lose themselves in the mist of half-sleep. Always they lay soft velvet fingers on the drowsy imagination, so that in their caressing you feel the vaster spaces from which they have come. Peaceful-brooding your *faculties* receive. Hearing, sight, smell—all are preternaturally keen to whatever of sound and sight and woods perfume is abroad through the night; and yet at the same time active appreciation dozes, so these things lie on it sweet and cloying like fallen rose-leaves.

Nothing is more fantastically unreal to tell about, nothing more concretely real to experience, than this undernote of the quick water. And when you do lie awake at night, it is always making its unobtrusive appeal. Gradually its hypnotic spell works. The distant chimes ring louder and nearer as you cross the borderland of sleep. And then outside the tent some little woods noise snaps the thread. An owl hoots, a whippoorwill cries, a twig cracks beneath the cautious prowl of some night creature—at once the yellow sunlit French meadows puff away—you are staring at the blurred image of the moon spraying through the texture of your tent.

You have cast from you with the warm blanket the drowsiness of dreams. A coolness, physical and spiritual, bathes you from head to foot. All your senses are keyed to the last vibrations. You hear the littler night prowlers; you glimpse the greater. A faint, searching woods perfume of dampness greets your nostrils. And somehow, mysteriously, in a manner not to be understood, the forces of the world seem in suspense, as though a touch might crystallize infinite possibilities into infinite power and motion. But the touch lacks. The forces hover on the edge of action, unheeding the little noises. In all humbleness and awe, you are a dweller of the Silent Places.

The night wind from the river, or from the open spaces of the wilds, chills you after a time. You begin to think of your blankets. In a few moments you roll yourself in their soft wool. Instantly it is morning.

And, strange to say, you have not to pay by going through the day unrefreshed. You may feel like turning in at eight instead of nine, and you may fall asleep with unusual promptitude, but your journey will begin clear-headedly, proceed springily, and end with much in reserve. No languor, no dull headache, no exhaustion, follows your experience. For this once your two hours of sleep have been as effective as nine.

9. In paragraph 2, "faculties" is used to mean
    a. teachers
    b. senses
    c. imaginations
    d. woods
    e. capacities

10. The author's opinion of insomnia is that
  a. it is not a problem because nights without sleep are refreshing
  b. it can happen more often when sleeping in the woods because of the noises in nature
  c. it is generally unpleasant, but sometimes can be hypnotic
  d. it is a terrible trial that can be caused by rashness or excitation
  e. it is the best way to cultivate imagination

11. By 'strange to say' in the final paragraph, the author most likely means
  a. the experience of the night before had an unreal quality
  b. the language used in describing the night before is not easily understood
  c. after a night like the one described, one awakens with supernatural capabilities
  d. it is not considered acceptable to express the opinion the author expresses
  e. contrary to expectations, one is well-rested after the night before

12. How is this essay best characterized?
  a. a playful examination of a common medical problem
  b. an erudite and scientific treatise
  c. a curious look at both sides of an issue
  d. a fanciful description of the author's experience
  e. a horrific depiction of night hallucinations

Questions 13 – 22 are based on the following passages:

Passage 1: An excerpt from the essay *Tradition and the Individual Talent* by T.S. Eliot (public domain):

No poet, no artist of any art, has his complete meaning alone. His significance, his appreciation is the appreciation of his relation to the dead poets and artists. You cannot value him alone; you must set him, for contrast and comparison, among the dead. I mean this as a principle of aesthetic, not merely historical, criticism. The necessity that he shall conform, that he shall cohere, is not one-sided; what happens when a new work of art is created is something that happens simultaneously to all the works of art which preceded it. The existing monuments form an ideal order among themselves, which is modified by the introduction of the new (the really new) work of art among them. The existing order is complete before the new work arrives; for order to persist after the supervention of novelty, the *whole* existing order must be, if ever so slightly, altered; and so the relations, proportions, values of each work of art toward the whole are readjusted; and this is conformity between the old and the new. Whoever has approved this idea of order, of the form of European, of English literature, will not find it preposterous that the past should be altered by the present as much as the present is directed by the past. And the poet who is aware of this will be aware of great difficulties and responsibilities.

Passage 2: An excerpt from the Clive Bell's seminal art history book <u>Art</u> (public domain):

To criticize a work of art historically is to play the science-besotted fool. No more disastrous theory ever issued from the brain of a charlatan than that of evolution in art. Giotto[1] did not creep, a grub, that Titian[2] might flaunt, a butterfly. To think of a man's art as leading on to the art of someone else is to misunderstand it. To praise or abuse or be interested in a work of art because it leads or does not lead to another work of art is to treat it as though it were not a work of art. The connection of one work of art with another may have everything to do with history: it has nothing to do with appreciation. So soon as we begin to consider a work as anything else than an end in itself we leave the world of art. Though the development of painting from Giotto to Titian may be interesting historically, it cannot affect the value of any particular picture: aesthetically, it is of no consequence whatever. Every work of art must be judged on its own merits.

13. In Passage 1, the word "cohere" is used to most closely mean
    a. to be congruous with
    b. to supplant
    c. to imitate
    d. to overhaul
    e. to deviate from

14. In Passage 1, the author uses "(the really new)" to mean which of the following?
    a. Art is subject to trends and fashions, which change constantly.
    b. Poets are always looking for new authors that have new ideas.
    c. The history of art has already been set and is not wavered by new artists.
    d. The past cannot be changed by the present, regardless of how modern present art is.
    e. Art has a narrative which can be modified by an idea which is entirely original.

---

[1] Giotto was an Italian painter during the Middle Ages.
[2] Titian was an Italian painter during the Renaissance.

15. In Passage 2, the author alludes to a butterfly to contradict which of the following concepts?
    a. The theory of evolution is responsible for the discipline of art criticism.
    b. Scientific knowledge is not necessary to understand paintings.
    c. Artists who show off are doomed to be criticized.
    d. Art which finds inspiration in nature is the highest form of art.
    e. Titian's art is beautiful as a result of the horrible art that came before.

16. The author of Passage 1 would be most likely to support:
    a. an artist who imitated the great works of the past
    b. an art critic who relied solely on evaluating the aesthetics of new art
    c. a historian who studied the aesthetic evolution of art
    d. an artist who was also a scientist
    e. an artist who shouldered the burden of creating something new to the world of art

17. Which of the following best describes the tone of Passage 1?
    a. polemic
    b. intimate
    c. infuriated
    d. sophisticated
    e. reactionary

18. In Passage 2, the word "charlatan" is used to refer to:
    a. leviathan
    b. amateur
    c. fraud
    d. scientist
    e. sculptor

19. The meaning of the sentence "To praise or abuse or be interested in a work of art because it leads or does not lead to another work of art is to treat it as though it were not a work of art" in Passage 2 means
    a. works of art cannot be judged primarily by their relation to one another
    b. one should not vandalize works of art
    c. it is necessary to understand how one work of art leads to another in order to judge it
    d. works of art must be treated with respect
    e. understanding works of art is reliant on seeing them on a historical scale

20. The author of Passage 1 would likely agree with which of the following statements?
    a. The past is a monument that is unalterable by the present.
    b. Historical knowledge is entirely separate from artistic knowledge.
    c. To understand a novel written in the twentieth century, it is necessary to have some knowledge of nineteenth century literature.
    d. Painters of Italian descent are all related to one another.
    e. One cannot be a scholar of literary history without also being a scholar of scientific thought.

21. The authors of Passage 1 and Passage 2 would likely come to consensus regarding which of the following statements?
    a. An aesthetic judgment is the greatest possible approach to art criticism.
    b. Knowledge of history compromises one's ability to criticize works of art.
    c. The painter Titian was able to create his art as a consequence of the art which came before his time.
    d. It is imperative to understand the progression from one work of art to another.
    e. Not all works of art are consequential.

22. Which of the following best describes the audiences for Passage 1 and Passage 2?
    a. Both Passage 1 and Passage 2 are directed to art historians.
    b. Passage 1 is directed to artists, while Passage 2 is directed to art critics.
    c. Passage 1 is directed to the author of Passage 2.
    d. Both passages are directed to young poets.
    e. Neither passage is directed to those who wish to understand art.

For the following questions, select the answer choice with the word or words that best fit in the sentence.

23. In order to ------ the tradition, the family members made an effort to ------ the younger generation in the way that they had done it in the past.
    a. nullify…assuage
    b. extend…indoctrinate
    c. formalize…assimilate
    d. deemphasize…edify
    e. perpetuate…instruct

24. The play had a ------ tone; all the patrons left the theater chortling and pleased.
    a. ecstatic
    b. jovial
    c. somber
    d. analytic
    e. melancholy

25. Jeff was absolutely ------ about his idea; try as we might, we could not dissuade him.
    a. parsimonious
    b. relenting
    c. adamant
    d. pragmatic
    e. capricious

26. In weaving cloth with threads, one draws the weft, or horizontal yarns, through the warp yarns, or the vertical, in an even and ------ manner to create a tight cloth.
    a. consistent
    b. oblique
    c. imaginative
    d. wholesome
    e. substantial

27. College students quickly learn that ------ can be much more valuable than ------; all the intelligence in the world does not help if you are not able to manage your time.
    a. perspicacity...ambition
    b. decorum...alacrity
    c. efficiency...aptitude
    d. accountability...solicitude
    e. wiliness...acumen

28. Clarissa was grateful for her friend's assistance with editing down her originally ------ acceptance speech.
    a. turgid
    b. mellifluous
    c. dilated
    d. laconic
    e. concise

29. "The party was an unmitigated disaster," Josephine said with ------, unworried about hurting anyone's feelings.
   a. barbarity
   b. vexation
   c. elation
   d. ire
   e. candor

30. The Natural History Museum had an extensive exhibit which explained how scientists were able to learn the habits of ------ mammals from the ------ remains of their bodies.
   a. extinct…ossified
   b. reserved…mummified
   c. omnivorous…decayed
   d. ambiguous…coded
   e. wary…petrified

31. Erin ------ the volume of the music coming through her headphones in an effort to ------ the conversation of the men sitting behind her on the bus.
   a. diminished…conceal
   b. terminated…transcribe
   c. maximized…amplify
   d. elevated…obstruct
   e. mitigated…fathom

32. It is our opinion that preventing others from accessing information that could be helpful to them is ------- act.
   a. a transient
   b. an exceptionable
   c. a tractable
   d. an irascible
   e. an egalitarian

Questions 33-34 are based on a short passage excerpted from "A Matter of Proportion" by Anne Walker, a short science-fiction story published in 1959 (public domain). In this excerpt, one character tells another about an injured man who is planning a secret operation.

On the way, he filled in background. Scott had been living out of the hospital in a small apartment, enjoying as much liberty as he could manage. He had equipment so he could stump around, and an antique car specially equipped. He wasn't complimentary about them. Orthopedic products had to be: unreliable, hard to service, unsightly, intricate, and uncomfortable. If they also squeaked and cut your clothes, fine!

Having to plan every move with an eye on weather and a dozen other factors, he developed an uncanny foresight. Yet he had to improvise at a moment's notice. With life a continuous high-wire act, he trained every surviving fiber to precision, dexterity, and tenacity. Finally, he avoided help. Not pride, self-preservation; the compulsively helpful have rarely the wit to ask before rushing in to knock you on your face, so he learned to bide his time till the horizon was clear of beaming simpletons. Also, he found an interest in how far he could go.

33. Why does Scott primarily avoid the help of others?
    a. He has found that he is usually better off without it.
    b. He does not want to rely on other people for anything.
    c. He is doing experiments to test his own limits.
    d. He is working on a secret operation and cannot risk discovery.
    e. He does not realize that he needs assistance.

34. "Orthopedic" in paragraph one most nearly means:
    a. uncomfortable
    b. dangerous
    c. corrective
    d. enhanced
    e. complicated

Questions 35-40 are based on a long passage excerpted from _Insects and Disease_ by Rennie W. Doane, a popular science account published in 1910 (public domain).

It has been estimated that there are about four thousand species or kinds of Protozoans, about twenty-five thousand species of mollusks, about ten thousand species of birds, about three thousand five hundred species of mammals, and from two hundred thousand to one million species of insects, or from two to five times as many kinds of insects as all other animals combined.

Not only do the insects preponderate in number of species, but the number of individuals belonging to many of the species is absolutely beyond our comprehension. Try to count the number of little green aphis on a single infested rose-bush, or on a cabbage plant; guess at the number of mosquitoes issuing each day from a good breeding-pond; estimate the number of scale insects on a single square inch of a tree badly infested with San José scale; then try to think how many more bushes or trees or ponds may be breeding their millions just as these and you will only begin to comprehend the meaning of this statement.

As long as these myriads of insects keep in what we are pleased to call their proper place we care not for their numbers and think little of them except as some student points out some wonderful thing about their structure, life-history or adaptations. But since the dawn of history we find accounts to show that insects have not always kept to their proper sphere but have insisted at various times and in various ways in interfering with man's plans and wishes, and on account of their excessive numbers the results have often been most disastrous.

Insects cause an annual loss to the people of the United States of over $1,000,000,000. Grain fields are devastated; orchards and gardens are destroyed or seriously affected; forests are made waste places and in scores of other ways these little pests which do not keep in their proper places are exacting this tremendous tax from our people. These things have been known and recognized for centuries, and scores of volumes have been written about the insects and their ways and of methods of combating them.

Yellow fever, while not so widespread as malaria, is more fatal and therefore more terrorizing. Its presence and spread are due entirely to a single species of mosquito, *Stegomyia calopus*. While this species is usually restricted to tropical or semi-tropical regions it sometimes makes its appearance in places farther north, especially in summer time, where it may thrive for a time. The adult mosquito is black, conspicuously marked with white. The legs and abdomen are banded with white and on the thorax is a series of white lines which in well-preserved specimens distinctly resembles a lyre. These mosquitoes are essentially domestic insects, for they are very rarely found except in houses or in their immediate vicinity. Once they enter a room they will scarcely leave it except to lay their eggs in a near-by cistern, water-pot, or some other convenient place.

Their habit of biting in the daytime has gained for them the name of "day mosquitoes" to distinguish them from the night feeders. But they will bite at night as well as by day and many other species are not at all adverse to a daylight meal, if the opportunity offers, so this habit is not distinctive. The recognition of these facts has a distinct bearing in the methods adopted to prevent the spread of yellow fever. There are no striking characters or habits in the larval or pupal stages that would enable us to distinguish without careful examination this species from other similar forms with which it might be associated. For some time it was claimed that this species would breed only in clean water, but it has been found that it is not nearly so particular, some even claiming that it prefers foul water. I have seen them breeding in countless thousands in company with *Stegomyia scutellaris* and *Culex fatigans* in the sewer drains in Tahiti in the streets of Papeete. As the larva feed largely on bacteria one would expect to find them in exactly such places where the bacteria are of course abundant. The fact that they are able to live in any kind of water and in a very small amount of it well adapts them to their habits of living about dwellings.

35. In paragraph 1, the author lists the amounts of different species of organisms in order to
    a. illustrate the vast number of species in the world
    b. demonstrate authority on the subject of insects
    c. establish the relative importance of mollusks and birds
    d. demonstrate the proportion of insects to other organisms
    e. refute prior scientific claims

36. What does the author mean by "their proper place" at the beginning of paragraph 2?
    a. The author feels that insects belong only outdoors.
    b. The author is demonstrating that insects should be studied carefully.
    c. The author wants the reader to feel superior to insects.
    d. The author is warning that insects can evolve to affect the course of human events.
    e. The author is alluding to people's tendency to view insects as largely irrelevant to their lives.

37. This passage can primarily be characterized as
    a. pedantic
    b. droll
    c. informative
    d. abstract
    e. cautionary

38. The main idea of this passage is best summarized as
    a. Disease-carrying mosquitoes have adapted to best live near human settlements.
    b. Insects can have a detrimental effect on the economy by destroying crops.
    c. Insects are numerous in both types of species and individuals within a species.
    d. Although people do not always consider insects consequential, they can have substantial effects on human populations.
    e. Prior scientific thought regarding insects has been largely fallacious.

39. The use of "domestic" in paragraph 5 most nearly means
    a. originating in the United States
    b. under the care of and bred by humans
    c. fearful of the outdoors
    d. devoted to home life
    e. living near human homes

40. Which of the following ideas would best belong in this passage?
   a. A historical example of the effect that a yellow fever outbreak had on civilization
   b. An biological explanation of how diseases are transmitted from insects to humans
   c. An examination of non-disease-carrying insects such as moths
   d. A reference to the numbers of insects that live far away from human habitation
   e. Strategies for the prevention of yellow fever and malaria

Questions 41-49 are based on a long original passage (author Elissa Yeates):

The collapse of the arbitrage[3] firm Long-Term Capital Management (LTCM) in 1998 is explained by a host of different factors: its investments were based on a high level of leverage, for example, and it was significantly impacted by Russia's default on the ruble. However, sociologist Donald MacKenzie maintains that the main factor in LTCM's demise was that, like all arbitrage firms, it was subjected to the sociological phenomena of the arbitrage community; namely, imitation. Arbitrageurs, who are generally known to one another as members of a specific subset of the financial society, use decision-making strategies based not only on mathematical models or pure textbook reason, but also based upon their feelings and gut reactions toward the financial market and on the actions of their peers. This imitation strategy leads to the overlapping "super portfolio," which creates an inherent instability that leads to collapse, the most infamous example being LTCM.

The public opinion of the partners of the firm in 1998 was that it had acted cavalierly with borrowed capital. However, in actuality the firm's strategy was exceedingly conservative, with a diversified portfolio, overestimated risks, and carefully hedged investments. The firm even tested tactics for dealing with financial emergencies such as the collapse of the European Monetary Union. Before the 1998 crisis, those in LTCM were never accused of recklessness. Nor were they, as is sometimes explained, overly reliant on mathematical models. The statistical hubris explanation falters under MacKenzie's evidence that John Meriwether and the others who ran the firm made their investment decisions based more upon their intricate understandings of the arbitrage market rather than upon the pure results of mathematical analyses. The financial instability that was created was not the result of the decision-making of one firm; but rather, the collective patterns of decision-making of all of the arbitrage firms at the time.

---

[3] "Arbitrage" is a financial strategy which takes advantage of the temporary price differences of a single asset in different markets.

The infamy of LTCM worked against the company. LTCM was composed of some of the most eminent minds in finance and it made devastating profits for the first few years that it was running. This led to imitation by other arbitrageurs who viewed the investments of LTCM as nearly sure bets. This type of replication of investment portfolios is not surprising, considering that arbitrageurs are all looking for similar types of pricing discrepancies and anomalies to exploit. The structure of arbitrageurs as a unique subset of the financial community who are largely personally known to one another further contributes to this phenomenon. Because of these factors over time the various players in the field of arbitrage created overlapping investments which MacKenzie dubs a "super portfolio." While LTCM alone may have created a geographically and industrially diverse portfolio, across the discipline of arbitrage as a whole capital flocked to similar investments.

Because of this super portfolio trend, multiple arbitrageurs were affected by the price changes of different assets caused by the actions of single independent firms. MacKenzie cites the example of the takeover of the investment bank Salomon Brothers by the Travelers Corporation. Salomon Brothers' portfolio, now under the management of someone who disliked the risks of arbitrage trading, liquidated its positions, which drove down the prices of assets in the markets in which it operated. The liquidation of the holdings of such a prominent player in the arbitrage game negatively affected the positions of every other firm that had a stake in those markets, including, of course, LTCM. This also illustrates the other sociological side of MacKenzie's argument: that arbitrageurs are subject to irrational internal pressures to cut their losses before their investments play out, which one of his interview subjects terms "queasiness" when faced with a stretch of losses.

41. The second paragraph of this passage primarily aims to
    a. explain that recklessness with borrowed capital is never profitable
    b. explore the factors ultimately responsible for the demise of the arbitrage firm Long-Term Capital Management
    c. demonstrate how the practice of arbitrage works
    d. laud the use of statistical models in calculating financial risks
    e. present and dismiss several theories of the collapse of Long-Term Capital Management

42. In paragraph two, "devastating" is used to mean
    a. destructive
    b. attractive
    c. blasphemous
    d. considerable
    e. appalling

43. The sociologist Donald McKenzie would likely agree with which of the following statements?
    a. Financial phenomena can be the result of human relationships rather than fluctuations in world markets.
    b. Long-Term Capital Management would not have collapsed if its investors had been less audacious.
    c. Arbitrageurs are known for acting independently from one another.
    d. The public well understood the factors that led to the demise of Long-Term Capital Management in 1998.
    e. Even within highly disciplined communities, there are always those who act irrationally.

44. The final paragraph in this passage
    a. refutes the argument presented in the second paragraph of the passage
    b. gives a logical example of the phenomenon described in the introductory first paragraph of the passage
    c. contains an ardent plea against the passage of arbitrage
    d. gives a step-by-step account of the demise of Long-Term Capital Management
    e. argues that an understanding of sociology is crucial to successful financial practice

45. Which of the following is a best description of the author's approach to the topic?
    a. impassioned exposition
    b. curious exploration
    c. gleeful detection
    d. disgusted condemnation
    e. serene indifference

46. Which of the following most accurately summarizes the author's thesis?
    a. If Long-Term Capital Management had developed a superportfolio, it would not have collapsed.
    b. Financial markets are inherently instable because those who participate in them are subject to human faults.
    c. Arbitrage firms should always endeavor to have geographically and industrially diverse investments.
    d. Long-Term Capital Management collapsed because arbitrageurs across the industry were investing in the same things, which caused instability.
    e. Long-Term Capital Management was run by financiers who were reckless and overly dependent on mathematical models, which is why it collapsed.

47. "Hubris" in paragraph two most likely means:
    a. mathematical model
    b. reliance
    c. arrogance
    d. denial
    e. mistake

48. Which of the following facts would undermine the main argument of the passage?
    a. The European Monetary Union was close to collapse in 1998.
    b. Some arbitrage firms steered clear of the practice of superportfolios.
    c. The Travelers Corporation was run by financiers who favored the practice of arbitrage.
    d. Arbitrageurs rarely communicate with one another or get information from the same source.
    e. Mathematical models used in finance in the 1990s were highly reliable.

49. Which of the following would support the argument made in the third paragraph of this passage?
    a. A detailed outline of the statistical models used by Long-Term Capital Management to make decisions.
    b. An explanation of how other arbitrage firms were able to learn the tactics practiced by Long-Term Capital Management.
    c. Examples of the differences between different investment portfolios of arbitrage firms.
    d. An outline of sociological theories about decision-making processes.
    e. A map showing the geographical diversity of arbitrage investors.

For the following questions, select the answer choice with the word or words that best fit in the sentence.

50. We ------ rejected the amendment; no argument or plea could persuade us to reverse our position.
    a. equivocally
    b. harmoniously
    c. lugubriously
    d. categorically
    e. ambiguously

51. Even though the latest tests had ------ an outbreak as a possibility, the ------ of the epidemic continued to frighten the research team.
    a. eliminated...ruse
    b. flourished...reprieve
    c. eradicated...specter
    d. delineated...chance
    e. subjugated...theory

52. The author was rarely intrigued by the ------ details of detective work; rather, he explored the exciting moments of danger and suspense.
    a. mundane
    b. anxious
    c. listless
    d. copious
    e. definitive

53. The introduction to the new edition of essays ------ the virtues of the author, who had won several literary prizes.
    a. impugned
    b. extolled
    c. revamped
    d. improvised
    e. desecrated

54. Given the limited resources available, it would not be ------ to ----- what we have.
    a. boorish...appropriate
    b. asinine...aggregate
    c. expedient...squander
    d. prudent...inhibit
    e. facetious...ruin

55. The fundraising dinner at the museum was attended by a ------ group of artists, business owners, students, socialites, and publishers.
    a. heterogeneous
    b. contentious
    c. stimulating
    d. prosaic
    e. outlandish

56. Niku refused to acknowledge the ------ in her opinion against the expansion of tourism while she herself invested in the ------ chain of hotels.
   a. duplicity…extravagant
   b. consistency…growing
   c. righteousness…declining
   d. hypocrisy…burgeoning
   e. relevance…lucrative

Questions 57 – 70 are based on a long passage excerpted from Robert Louis Stevenson's classic novel Treasure Island (public domain). In this passage, the narrator tells about an old sailor staying at his family's inn.

He had taken me aside one day and promised me a silver fourpenny on the first of every month if I would only keep my "weather-eye open for a seafaring man with one leg" and let him know the moment he appeared. Often enough when the first of the month came round and I applied to him for my wage, he would only blow through his nose at me and stare me down, but before the week was out he was sure to think better of it, bring me my fourpenny piece, and repeat his orders to look out for "the seafaring man with one leg."

How that personage haunted my dreams, I need scarcely tell you. On stormy nights, when the wind shook the four corners of the house and the surf roared along the cove and up the cliffs, I would see him in a thousand forms, and with a thousand diabolical expressions. Now the leg would be cut off at the knee, now at the hip; now he was a monstrous kind of a creature who had never had but the one leg, and that in the middle of his body. To see him leap and run and pursue me over hedge and ditch was the worst of nightmares. And altogether I paid pretty dear for my monthly fourpenny piece, in the shape of these abominable fancies.

But though I was so terrified by the idea of the seafaring man with one leg, I was far less afraid of the captain himself than anybody else who knew him. There were nights when he took a deal more rum and water than his head would carry; and then he would sometimes sit and sing his wicked, old, wild sea-songs, minding nobody; but sometimes he would call for glasses round and force all the trembling company to listen to his stories or bear a chorus to his singing. Often I have heard the house shaking with "Yo-ho-ho, and a bottle of rum," all the neighbors joining in for dear life, with the fear of death upon them, and each singing louder than the other to avoid remark. For in these fits he was the most overriding companion ever known; he would slap his hand on the table for silence all round; he would fly up in a passion of anger at a question, or sometimes because none was put, and so he judged the company was not following his story. Nor would he allow anyone to leave the inn till he had drunk himself sleepy and reeled off to bed.

His stories were what frightened people worst of all. Dreadful stories they were—about hanging, and walking the plank, and storms at sea, and the Dry Tortugas, and wild deeds and places on the Spanish Main. By his own account he must have lived his life among some of the wickedest men that God ever allowed upon the sea, and the language in which he told these stories shocked our plain country people almost as much as the crimes that he described. My father was always saying the inn would be ruined, for people would soon cease coming there to be tyrannized over and put down, and sent shivering to their beds; but I really believe his presence did us good. People were frightened at the time, but on looking back they rather liked it; it was a fine excitement in a quiet country life, and there was even a party of the younger men who pretended to admire him, calling him a "true sea-dog" and a "real old salt" and such like names, and saying there was the sort of man that made England terrible at sea.

In one way, indeed, he bade fair to ruin us, for he kept on staying week after week, and at last month after month, so that all the money had been long exhausted, and still my father never plucked up the heart to insist on having more. If ever he mentioned it, the captain blew through his nose so loudly that you might say he roared, and stared my poor father out of the room. I have seen him wringing his hands after such a rebuff, and I am sure the annoyance and the terror he lived in must have greatly hastened his early and unhappy death.

57. What does the phrase "that personage" reference at the beginning of Paragraph 2?
    a. the old sailor staying at the inn
    b. the narrator's father
    c. the seafaring man with one leg
    d. a sailor from the Spanish Main
    e. a neighbor

58. The purpose of Paragraph 3 is to
    a. illustrate how others view the captain
    b. explain the narrator's relationship with the captain
    c. give more background information about the inn where the narrator lives
    d. recount old seafaring lore
    e. explain why the captain is staying at this inn

59. The tone of the first sentence in Paragraph 2 ("How that personage haunted…") is
    a. dreamlike
    b. confessional
    c. amused
    d. horrified
    e. intimate

60. Which paragraph serves to evoke the life lived by sailors at sea?
    a. 1
    b. 2
    c. 3
    d. 4
    e. 5

61. "Diabolical" in Paragraph 2 most nearly means
    a. angry
    b. judgmental
    c. contorted
    d. fiendish
    e. stoic

62. What kind of character does the author reveal the captain to be the third paragraph?
    a. temperamental
    b. generous
    c. jocund
    d. mysterious
    e. reserved

63. What does the author reveal about the narrator in Paragraph 5?
    a. The narrator is afraid of the captain.
    b. The narrator is eager to go to sea.
    c. The narrator was often angry and annoyed.
    d. The narrator grew up in poverty.
    e. The narrator lost his father at an early age.

64. What does the narrator mean by "I paid pretty dear for my monthly fourpenny piece" at the end of Paragraph 2?
    a. He had to give the captain a valuable coin each month to preserve his safety.
    b. He earned the fourpenny by keeping a watch for the man with one leg, which gave him terrible nightmares.
    c. He had to pay with a fourpenny coin each month to stay at this inn.
    d. He had to stay up all night keeping watch to earn the coin, which ended up causing him problems.
    e. By accepting the captain's fourpenny piece, the narrator created a problematic friendship with him.

65. "Tyrannized" in Paragraph 4 is used to mean
    a. cajoled
    b. bullied
    c. frightened
    d. robbed
    e. ejected

66. Which of the following statements about this passage is false?
    a. It is unclear whether the "seafaring man with one leg" actually exists.
    b. The narrator harbors a serious grudge against the captain.
    c. The narrator is interested in the captain's stories.
    d. The story takes place near the ocean.
    e. Most people who populate the story are afraid of the captain.

67. The phrase "in a thousand forms, and with a thousand diabolical expressions" is an example of which literary device?
    a. hyperbole
    b. metaphor
    c. foreshadowing
    d. allegory
    e. symbolism

68. According to the captain, all of the following are hazards which can be encountered at sea EXCEPT
    a. hangings
    b. wicked men
    c. walking the plank
    d. storms
    e. sea monsters

69. It can be inferred from the passage that
    a. Singing was frowned upon in the community
    b. The narrator never knew his mother
    c. The narrator admired the captain
    d. The captain is afraid of the seafaring man with one leg
    e. The narrator went on to become a pirate

70. By "they rather liked it" at the end of Paragraph 4, the author most closely means
    a. the patrons of the inn enjoyed singing
    b. the captain and others appreciated the rum available for sale at the inn
    c. the narrator and his friends liked the stories the captain told
    d. the captain provided entertainment at the inn, which would otherwise be boring
    e. the narrator's parents liked having the captain around

Questions 71 – 74 are based on a short passage excerpted from the introduction to The Best American Humorous Short Stories, edited by Alexander Jessup (public domain).

No book is duller than a book of jokes, for what is refreshing in small doses becomes nauseating when perused in large assignments. Humor in literature is at its best not when served merely by itself but when presented along with other ingredients of literary force in order to give a wide representation of life. Therefore "professional literary humorists," as they may be called, have not been much considered in making up this collection. In the history of American humor there are three names which stand out more prominently than all others before Mark Twain, who, however, also belongs to a wider classification: "Josh Billings" (Henry Wheeler Shaw, 1815-1885), "Petroleum V. Nasby" (David Ross Locke, 1833-1888), and "Artemus Ward" (Charles Farrar Browne, 1834-1867). In the history of American humor these names rank high; in the field of American literature and the American short story they do not rank so high. I have found nothing of theirs that was first-class both as humor and as short story. Perhaps just below these three should be mentioned George Horatio Derby (1823-1861), author of *Phoenixiana* (1855) and the *Squibob Papers* (1859), who wrote under the name "John Phoenix." As has been justly said, "Derby, Shaw, Locke and Browne carried to an extreme numerous tricks already invented by earlier American humorists, particularly the tricks of gigantic exaggeration and calm-faced mendacity, but they are plainly in the main channel of American humor, which had its origin in the first comments of settlers upon the conditions of the frontier, long drew its principal inspiration from the differences between that frontier and the more settled and compact regions of the country, and reached its highest development in Mark Twain, in his youth a child of the American frontier, admirer and imitator of Derby and Browne, and eventually a man of the world and one of its greatest humorists."

71. The author of this passage would disagree with all of the following statements EXCEPT:
    a. To be a successful storyteller, one must also be a professional literary humorist.
    b. Mark Twain is the most prominent American humorist.
    c. Lying with a straight face is a literary humorist device which had just been invented at the time this was published.
    d. The best joke books are the longest ones.
    e. Professional literary humorism is the highest form of writing.

72. The purpose of this passage is to
    a. scorn humorous writing as lesser than storytelling.
    b. explain how writers use humorous literary devices.
    c. provide contextual information about the landscape of American humorous writing.

> d. make a case for the appreciation of the humorists Henry Shaw and David Locke.
>
> e. deny the historical roots of American literary humor

73. The word "prominently" in line four most closely means
    a. extravagantly
    b. inconspicuously
    c. significantly
    d. comically
    e. conceitedly

74. Which of the following best summarizes the author's theory of the origins of American humorous writing?
    a. It started as a way of breaking away from British literary humor.
    b. It grew hand-in-hand with American storytelling.
    c. It was founded by Mark Twain.
    d. It was inspired by the differences between settlements and the frontier.
    e. It began with exaggerations and mendacity.

For the following questions, select the answer choice with the word or words that best fit in the sentence.

75. ------ with the law was to be expected, as the penalties for defying it were very harsh.
    a. Quibbling
    b. Evading
    c. Compliance
    d. Defiance
    e. Compromising

76. Even though his parents showed him otherwise, the child kept crying and ----- insisting that there was a monster in the hallway.
    a. emphatically
    b. blithely
    c. agreeably
    d. facetiously
    e. amicably

77. It took years before the auditor's ------ was revealed: she was found to be helping others hide their financial ------.
    a. proficiency…archives
    b. innocence…deception
    c. fraud…exertion
    d. duplicity…wrongdoing
    e. inadequacy…misdeed

78. The actress was possessed of superb ------: she was constantly approached to record audiobooks.
   a. elocution
   b. agility
   c. pulchritude
   d. pantomime
   e. decorum

79. Warren was able to ------ our disparate ideas into one ------, logical story.
   a. distill…irrational
   b. transmute…consistent
   c. fragment…lucid
   d. attenuate…cogent
   e. reorganize…preposterous

80. One of the ------ rules of our classroom is that we do not ------ the ideas of others; we want to have a place where everyone's thoughts are respected.
   a. cardinal…disparage
   b. negligible…insult
   c. wry…ignore
   d. rare…endorse
   e. copious…neglect

81. One of the characteristics ------ to my family is the ability to quickly adjust to any situation; my sisters, my father, and I are all this way.
   a. antipodal
   b. alien
   c. endemic
   d. contrary
   e. atypical

82. Because Aliyah volunteered us for the event, the ------ was on her to come up with the idea for our booth.
   a. remedy
   b. potential
   c. accolade
   d. stipulation
   e. onus

Critical Reading Section- Answers

1. B – prescient – having knowledge of things or events before they happen; having foresight
2. A – equatorial…impervious – typical of the regions at the earth's equator…not permitting penetration or passage
3. D – systematizing…digitized - making systematic, arranging in a system…converting to digital form
4. C – pretext – something put forward to conceal a true purpose
5. C – abrogate – to abolish by formal or official means
6. E – zest…undermined – an agreeable flavor imparted to something…to injure or destroy something by stages
7. D – holistically – incorporating the principle that whole entities have an existence greater than the sum of their parts
8. A – precise…deduced – operating with total accuracy…arrived at a conclusion from something known; to infer
9. B
10. C
11. E
12. D
13. A
14. E
15. E
16. E
17. D
18. C
19. A
20. C
21. E
22. B
23. E – perpetuate…instruct – to preserve from extinction…to furnish with knowledge
24. B – jovial – characterized by a hearty, joyous humor
25. C – adamant – utterly unyielding in attitude or opinion despite all appeals
26. A – consistent – steady; even
27. C – efficiency…aptitude – the production of desired effects with minimum waste of time or effort…inherent ability; intelligence
28. A – turgid – swollen; pompous
29. E – candor – openness; honesty
30. A – extinct…ossified – no longer in existence…the calcification of soft tissue into bonelike material
31. D – elevated…obstruct – raised…block out
32. B – an exceptionable – objectionable
33. A

34. C – corrective – orthopedic products are those designed to correct or ameliorate a medical condition
35. D
36. E
37. C
38. D
39. E
40. A
41. E
42. D
43. A
44. B
45. B
46. D
47. C
48. D
49. B
50. D – categorically – without exceptions or conditions; absolute
51. C – eradicated…specter – removed or destroyed utterly…some object or source of terror or dread
52. A – mundane – common; ordinary; banal
53. B – extolled – praised lavishly
54. C – expedient…squander – suitable or wise under the circumstance…use wastefully
55. A – heterogeneous – different in kind, unlike; incongruous
56. D – hypocrisy…burgeoning - pretense of morality that one does not really possess…growing or developing quickly
57. C
58. A
59. E
60. D
61. D
62. A
63. E
64. B
65. B
66. B
67. A
68. E
69. C
70. D
71. B
72. C
73. C
74. D

75. C – compliance – cooperation or obedience
76. A – emphatically – forceful, insistent
77. D – duplicity…wrongdoing – deceitfulness…the act of doing something immoral or illegal
78. A – elocution – manner of speaking and oral delivery
79. B – transmute…consistent – transform…compatible, not contradictory
80. A – cardinal…disparage – prime, chief…to slight or belittle
81. C – endemic – natural to or characteristic of
82. E – onus - responsibility

Chapter 9: Writing Section Question Bank

For questions 1 – 11, select the best segment to replace the underlined segment of the sentence.

1. Rod cells are found in the human <u>eye so they can absorb light to see in even dim environments</u>.
    a. eye, but can absorb light to see in even dim environments.
    b. eye to see in dim environments even by absorbing light.
    c. eye and can absorb light to see in even dim environments.
    d. eye and are absorbing light to see in even dim environments.
    e. eye so they can absorb light to see in even dim environments.

2. Having already finished her essay, <u>washing the truck was the thing Maricela was ready to do</u>.
    a. washing the truck was the next thing Maricela did.
    b. Maricela had another thing she was ready to do and that was washing the truck.
    c. washing the truck Maricela was ready to do.
    d. Maricela was ready to wash the truck.
    e. washing the truck was the thing Maricela was ready to do.

3. The information gathered from the national census <u>is used to determine political boundaries, inform policies, and planning transportation systems</u>.
    a. is used to determine political boundaries, inform policies, and plan transportation systems
    b. determines political boundaries and informs policies and plans transportation systems
    c. is determining political boundaries, informing policies, and planning transportation systems
    d. is used to determine political boundaries, informing policies, and planning transportation systems
    e. is used to determine political boundaries, inform policies, and planning transportation systems

4. Many artists and producers disagree over how copyright laws <u>should be applied, they have different perspectives</u> on what best protects and encourages creativity.
    a. should be applied since it is that they have different perspectives
    b. are applied with different perspectives
    c. should apply on differing perspectives
    d. are applied because they have different perspectives
    e. should be applied, they have different perspectives

5. Many consider television shows <u>to be eroding of our nation's imaginations and attention spans</u>.
   a. to erode our nation's imaginations and attention spans
   b. erosion of our nation's imaginations and attention spans
   c. to be eroding of our national imaginations and attention spans
   d. to be eroding of the national imagination and attention span
   e. to be eroding our nation's imaginations and attention spans

6. In the early 1960's, the Civil Rights movement in the United States <u>has swiftly grown to encompass</u> such movements as the Freedom Rides and the integration of universities.
   a. has grown swiftly to encompass
   b. has swiftly grown, encompassing
   c. growing swiftly has encompassed
   d. had swiftly grown to encompass
   e. has swiftly grown to encompass

7. Raul, the most knowledgeable of us all regarding physics, <u>maintain that we would be needing</u> better equipment.
   a. maintaining that we would need
   b. maintains that we would be needing
   c. maintains that we would need
   d. maintain we would have needed
   e. maintain that we would be needing

8. <u>Does anyone have an informed guess that they would like</u> to share before I reveal the answer?
   a. Do anyone have an informed guess that they would like
   b. Is anyone having an informed guess that they would like
   c. Does anyone have an informed guess that they are wanting
   d. Anyone with an informed guess would like
   e. Does anyone have an informed guess that they would like

9. <u>The meals at this restaurant have so much more salt in them than the restaurant we went to last week</u>.
   a. The meals at this restaurant have so much more salt in them than that other restaurant.
   b. The meals at this restaurant are so much saltier than the restaurant we went to last week.
   c. The meals at this restaurant have much more salt in them than the restaurant we went to last week.
   d. The meals at this restaurant have so much more salt in them than those at the restaurant we went to last week.
   e. The meals at this restaurant have so much more salt in them than the restaurant we went to last week.

10. Malaria is a mosquito-borne infectious disease <u>which can be prevented by taking a drug such as doxycycline, eradication of mosquitoes in areas inhabited by people, using mosquito nets to prevent the insects from entering homes, or a combination of these methods.</u>
    a. disease which can be prevented by taking a drug such as doxycycline, eradicating mosquitoes in areas inhabited by people, using mosquito nets to prevent the insects from entering homes, or a combination of these methods.
    b. disease that can only be prevented by taking a drug such as doxycycline, eradication of mosquitoes in areas inhabited by people, using mosquito nets to prevent the insects from entering homes, or a combination of these methods.
    c. disease which can be prevented by taking a drug such as doxycycline, eradication of mosquitoes in areas inhabited by people, use of mosquito nets to prevent the insects from entering homes, or a combination of these methods.
    d. disease which can be prevented by taking a drug such as doxycycline, eradication of mosquitoes in areas inhabited by people, using mosquito nets to prevent the insects from entering homes, and a combination of these methods.
    e. disease which can be prevented by taking a drug such as doxycycline, eradication of mosquitoes in areas inhabited by people, using mosquito nets to prevent the insects from entering homes, or a combination of these methods.

11. The Bernina Range <u>runs along eastern Switzerland and is considered to be a part of the</u> Central Eastern Alps.
    a. is running along eastern Switzerland and is considered to be a part of the
    b. runs along eastern Switzerland and is considered part of
    c. run along eastern Switzerland, consider to be a part of the
    d. run along eastern Switzerland and is considered to be a part of the
    e. runs along eastern Switzerland and is considered to be a part of the

The following sentences contain either one error or no errors. For questions 12 through 29, select the underlined section that contains the error, or select "E" for "no error."

12. When cooking with hot <u>oil it is prudent</u> for <u>one to wear</u> long sleeves, you do not want the oil to <u>splatter onto</u> your arms and burn <u>them</u>.

    a. oil it is prudent
    b. one to wear
    c. splatter onto
    d. them
    e. No error

13. <u>Jordan and I</u> practiced our show <u>over and over;</u> we <u>would have</u> only twenty minutes to play and we wanted to make sure <u>to play</u> our best songs.
    a. Jordan and I
    b. over and over;
    c. would have
    d. to play
    e. No error

14. Aliyah asked <u>Timothy and I</u> to help her run the student <u>election</u>, so this week <u>we are hanging</u> posters, printing the ballots, <u>and editing speeches</u>.
    a. Timothy and I
    b. election
    c. we are hanging
    d. and editing speeches
    e. No error

15. The <u>difficulty with navigating</u> subway systems <u>are compounded</u> <u>when some</u> stations are closed for <u>repair</u>.
    a. difficulty with navigating
    b. are compounded
    c. when some
    d. repair
    e. No error

16. We <u>were given</u> explicit instructions for how to deal with <u>this exact</u> situation: we are to <u>immediately halt</u> production <u>and be contacting</u> the supervisor.
    a. were given
    b. this exact
    c. to immediately halt
    d. and be contacting
    e. No error

17. The way the <u>shadows play</u> across the leaves <u>provide the artist</u> with <u>innumerable</u> challenges in painting the <u>twilit landscape</u>.
    a. shadows play
    b. provide the artist
    c. innumerable
    d. the twilit landscape
    e. No error

18. <u>Along the banks</u> of the Colorado River <u>grow many different kinds</u> of bushes and trees <u>which serve</u> as habitats for the deer mice, raccoons, jackrabbits, and toads <u>who live there</u>.
    a. Along the banks
    b. grow many different kinds
    c. which serve
    d. who live there
    e. No error

19. Gerald <u>slung his arm</u> about me <u>very</u> <u>familiar although</u> we had <u>only met hours ago</u>.
    a. slung his arm
    b. very
    c. familiar although
    d. only met hours ago
    e. No error

20. After hiking <u>all afternoon</u> in the rocky desert, <u>we had</u> desperate <u>need of</u> water bottles and <u>long, soothing showers.</u>
    a. all afternoon
    b. we had
    c. need of
    d. long, soothing showers
    e. No error

21. It took nearly <u>half an hour</u> to dish out the meals to the large group: first, we had to <u>give everyone food,</u> and then we had to make sure <u>that everyone got</u> <u>their beverage</u> as well.
    a. half an hour
    b. give everyone food
    c. that everyone got
    d. their beverage
    e. No error

22. When considering <u>what kind of</u> car to purchase, it is important to <u>factor in hidden costs</u> such as how much gas <u>the car consumed</u> and how expensive <u>maintenance will be</u>.
   a. what kind of
   b. factor in hidden costs
   c. the car consumed
   d. maintenance will be
   e. No error

23. Just before <u>the guests arrived</u> we realized that <u>we were going</u> to run out of paper plates, so <u>her and David</u> went to the store to buy <u>some</u>.
   a. the guests arrived
   b. we were going
   c. her and David
   d. some
   e. No error

24. <u>Regardless by</u> how much one <u>likes or appreciates</u> a gift, it is <u>absolutely necessary</u> to thank the giver in person, by telephone, <u>or preferably with</u> a card.
   a. Regardless by
   b. likes or appreciates
   c. absolutely necessary
   d. or preferably with
   e. No error

25. Even though Alaina <u>was generally cautious</u> when it came to daring physical feats, she was excited <u>to try</u> spelunking for the first time; <u>she'd heard</u> that <u>the caves were</u> breathtaking.
   a. was generally cautious
   b. to try
   c. she'd heard
   d. the caves were
   e. No error

26. The <u>borders of</u> Rasco County <u>is comprised</u> of the river to the north <u>and east</u> and interstates <u>along the south</u> and the west.
   a. borders of
   b. is comprised
   c. and east
   d. along the south
   e. No error

27. Each <u>applicant for</u> the open time slot <u>was asked</u> to give <u>their opinion on</u> the best way to improve the radio <u>station's programming</u>.
   a. applicant for
   b. was asked
   c. their opinion on
   d. station's programming
   e. No error

28. There <u>will likely never</u> be a general <u>consensus on</u> which <u>is best</u>: the sunrise <u>or</u> the sunset.
   a. will likely never
   b. consensus on
   c. is best
   d. or
   e. No error

29. The storm drew <u>menacing</u> near the town <u>where</u> citizens <u>had been</u> warned to move down to <u>their</u> cellars.
   a. menacing
   b. where
   c. had been
   d. their
   e. No error

Questions 30 – 35 are writing questions based on the following original passage. Sentences are numbered at the end for easy reference within the questions.

Examining the impact my lifestyle has on the earth's resources is, I believe, a fascinating and valuable thing to do (1). According to the Earth Day Network ecological footprint calculator, it would take four planet earths to sustain the human population if everyone used as many resources as I do (2). My "ecological footprint," or the amount of productive area of the earth that is required to produce the resources I consume, is therefore larger than the footprints of most of the population (3). It is hard to balance the luxuries and opportunities I have available to me with doing what I know to be better from an ecological standpoint (4).

It is fairly easy for me to recycle, so I do it, but it would be much harder to forgo the opportunity to travel by plane or eat my favorite fruits that have been flown to the supermarket from a different country (5). Although I get ecological points for my recycling habits, my use of public transportation, and living in an apartment complex rather than a free-standing residence, <u>my footprint expands when it is taken into account my not-entirely-local diet</u>, my occasional use of a car, my three magazine subscriptions, and my history of flying more than ten hours a year (6). I feel that realizing just how unfair my share of the earth's resources have been should help me to change at least some of my bad habits (7).

30. Which of the following is the best version of sentence 1?
   a. It is fascinating and valuable to examine the impact my lifestyle has on the earth's resources.
   b. Examining the impact my lifestyle has on the earth's resources is a fascinating and valuable thing to do.
   c. To examine the impact my lifestyle has on the earth's resources is fascinating and is also valuable.
   d. The impact of my lifestyle on the earth's resources is fascinating and valuable to examine.
   e. Examining the impact my lifestyle has on the earth's resources is, I believe, a fascinating and valuable thing to do.

31. How could sentences 2 and 3 best be combined?
   a. According to the Earth Day Network ecological footprint calculator, it would take four planet earths to sustain the human population if everyone used as many resources as I do because I have a very large "ecological footprint," which is the amount of productive area of the earth that is required to produce the resources I consume.
   b. According to the Earth Day Network ecological footprint calculator, which calculates the amount of productive area of the earth that is required to produce the resources one consumes, it would take four planet earths to sustain the human population if everyone had a footprint as large as mine.
   c. According to the Earth Day Network ecological footprint calculator, it would take four planet earths to sustain the human population if everyone used as many resources as I do; my "ecological footprint," or the amount of productive area of the earth that is required to produce the resources I consume, is therefore larger than the footprints of most of the population.
   d. According to the Earth Day Network ecological footprint calculator, which measures the amount of productive area of the earth that is required to produce the resources a person consumes, my footprint is larger than that of most: it would take four planet earths to sustain the human population if everyone consumed as much as I do.
   e. According to the Earth Day Network ecological footprint calculator, my "ecological footprint," or the amount of productive area of the earth that is required to produce the resources I consume, would require four planet earths if it were to be the footprint of the human population; it is therefore larger than the footprints of most of the population.

32. Sentence 4 would best fit if it were moved where in this composition?
   a. At the beginning of paragraph 2
   b. After sentence 5
   c. After sentence 6

    d. At the end of paragraph 2

    e. Sentence 4 is best left where it is.

33. Which two sentences would be improved by switching positions?
    a. 1 and 2
    b. 3 and 4
    c. 5 and 6
    d. 6 and 7
    e. 2 and 7

34. Which of the following should replace the underlined portion of sentence 6?
    a. my footprint expands when one takes into account my not-entirely-local diet
    b. my footprint expands when taken into account are my not-entirely-local diet
    c. my footprint expands when we take into account my not-entirely-local diet
    d. my footprint expands when it takes into account my not-entirely-local diet
    e. my footprint expands when it is taken into account my not-entirely-local diet

35. Which revision would most improve sentence 7?
    a. Eliminate the phrase "I feel that"
    b. Change "should help me" to "will help me"
    c. Add the phrase "In conclusion," to the beginning
    d. Change "have been" to "has been"
    e. Eliminate the phrase "at least some of"

For questions 36-50, select the best segment to replace the underlined segment of the sentence.

36. Wangari Maathai, whom I greatly admire, was given the Nobel Peace Prize in 2004 and was the first African woman to do so.
    a. the first African woman to win the Nobel Peace Prize, was given it in 2004 and I greatly admire her.
    b. who won the Nobel Peace Prize in 2004 and whom I greatly admire, was the first African woman to do so.
    c. whom I greatly admire, was the first African woman to win the Nobel Peace Prize, which she did in 2004.
    d. who was given the Nobel Peace Prize in 2004 and was the first African woman to do so, I greatly admire.
    e. whom I greatly admire, was given the Nobel Peace Prize in 2004 and was the first African woman to do so.

37. Even though she knew it would reflect badly on her polls, the politician withdrawing her statement.
    a. the politician is withdrawing her statement.
    b. the politician withdraws her statement.
    c. the politician was going to withdraw her statement.
    d. the politician withdrew her statement.
    e. the politician withdrawing her statement.

38. The holiday Cinco de Mayo is a Mexican-American tradition which celebrates the Mexican repulsion of the French occupation.
    a. tradition, celebrates the Mexican repulsion of the French occupation.
    b. tradition is celebrating the Mexican repulsion of the French occupation.
    c. celebration of the Mexican repulsion of the French occupation.
    d. celebrating of the Mexican repulsion of the French occupation.
    e. tradition which celebrates the Mexican repulsion of the French occupation.

39. Gazing out the window at the view of the mountains, the long car ride passed quickly for Mariah.
    a. passed quickly Mariah's long car ride.
    b. Mariah felt the long car ride passed quickly.
    c. Mariah quickly passing the long car ride.
    d. the long car ride was quickly passing for Mariah.
    e. the long car ride passed quickly for Mariah.

40. Parat reorganized all of the books in this section, it took him an afternoon.
    a. which was taking him an afternoon.
    b. taking him an afternoon.
    c. throughout the afternoon.
    d. a task that took an afternoon.
    e. it took him an afternoon.

41. The team of biologists submitted their findings to a peer-reviewed journal, a process that took months to complete.
    a. The team of biologists who submitted their findings to a peer-reviewed journal
    b. The team, of biologists, submitted their findings to a peer-reviewed journal
    c. The team of biologists submitted their findings in a peer-reviewed journal
    d. The team of biologists will submit their findings to a peer-reviewed journal
    e. The team of biologists submitted their findings to a peer-reviewed journal

42. We reached the summit of the mountain and, awestruck, <u>was looking out at the incredible view when the thunderstorm began</u>.
     a. were looking out at the incredible view when the thunderstorm began.
     b. looked out at the incredible view when the thunderstorm began.
     c. were in the middle of looking out at the incredible view when the thunderstorm began.
     d. were having looked out at the incredible view when the thunderstorm began.
     e. was looking out at the incredible view when the thunderstorm began.

43. <u>A spiral galaxy primarily consists of a flat, rotating disc of stars that is flat across space with one central bulge of stars</u>.
     a. A spiral galaxy is primarily consisting of a flat, rotating disc of stars that is flat across space with one central bulge of stars.
     b. A spiral galaxy primarily consists of a flat, rotating disc of stars with one central bulge of stars that is flat across space.
     c. A spiral galaxy primarily consists of a rotating disc of stars that is flat across space with one central bulge of stars.
     d. A spiral galaxy primarily consists of a flat, rotating disc of stars that is flat across space and has one central bulge of stars.
     e. A spiral galaxy primarily consists of a flat, rotating disc of stars that is flat across space with one central bulge of stars.

44. <u>The committee, which was formed by the governor's office, have one week to make a decision</u>.
     a. The committee formed by the governor's office have one week to make a decision.
     b. The committee formed by the governor's office are making the decision in one week.
     c. The committee, which was formed by the governor's office, are making the decision in one week.
     d. The committee, which was formed by the governor's office, has one week to make a decision.
     e. The committee, which was formed by the governor's office, have one week to make a decision.

45. The ocelot, a species of wild cat, <u>is one of the mammals that can be found across</u> both continents of the Americas.
     a. are one of the mammals that can be found across
     b. is a mammal that can be found across
     c. is one of the mammals that is found in
     d. are mammals that can be found across
     e. is one of the mammals that can be found across

46. <u>Every time you send her a letter</u>, Anita was so happy to receive it.
    a. Every time you sent her a letter
    b. Each time you send her a letter
    c. Every time one sends her a letter
    d. Every time you send her letters
    e. Every time you send her a letter

47. If you have <u>questions about the course schedule, please be seeing your counselor</u>.
    a. any questions regarding the course schedule, please be seeing your counselor.
    b. to ask the counselor your questions about the course schedule.
    c. questions about the course schedule, please see your counselor.
    d. a question about the course schedule, be seeing your counselor.
    e. questions about the course schedule, please be seeing your counselor.

48. To summarize a story, <u>it is necessary to consider the characters, the setting, and the conflict of them</u>.
    a. it is necessary to consider the characters, the setting, and the conflict of it.
    b. you have to consider the characters, the setting, and the conflict of them.
    c. it is necessary to be considerate of the characters, the setting, and the conflict of them.
    d. it is necessary to consider the characters, setting, and conflict of them.
    e. it is necessary to consider the characters, the setting, and the conflict of them.

49. Tina and Marie <u>had never seen anyone eating so loud; they were appalled</u>.
    a. had never seen anyone eating so loud and they were appalled.
    b. had never seen anyone eating so loudly; they were appalled.
    c. never saw anyone eating so loud; they were appalled.
    d. had never seen someone eating so loud; they were appalled.
    e. had never seen anyone eating so loud; they were appalled.

50. <u>It is so easy to be self-published these days; it seems as though everyone has a blog</u>.
    a. It is too easy to be self-published these days; it seems as though everyone has a blog.
    b. It is so easy to be self-published these days because it seems as though everyone has a blog.
    c. It is so easy to publish yourself these days; it seems as though everyone has a blog.
    d. It is so easy to be self-published these days; it seems as though everyone had a blog.

e. It is so easy to be self-published these days; it seems as though everyone has a blog.

Questions 51 – 56 are based on the short passage below, which is excerpted from Thomas Huxley's preface to his Collected Essays: Volume V (public domain) and modified slightly. Sentences are numbered at the end for easy reference within the questions.

I had set out on a journey, with no other purpose than that of exploring a certain province of natural knowledge, I strayed no hair's breadth from the course which it was my right and my duty to pursue; and yet I found that, whatever route I took, before long, I came to a tall and formidable-looking fence (1). Confident I might be in the existence of an ancient and indefeasible right of way, before me stood the thorny barrier with its comminatory notice-board—"No Thoroughfare. By order" (2). There seemed no way over; nor did the prospect of creeping round, as I saw some do, attracts me (3). True there was no longer any cause to fear the spring guns and man-traps set by former lords of the manor; but one is apt to get very dirty going on all-fours (4). The only alternatives were either to give up my journey—which I was not minded to do—or to break the fence down and go through it (5). I swiftly ruled out crawling under as an option (6). I also ruled out turning back (7).

51. How could sentence 1 best be changed?
   a. The comma after journey should be removed
   b. The comma after knowledge should be changed to a semicolon
   c. "and yet" should be eliminated
   d. Change "I had set out" to "I set out"
   e. No change

52. Sentence 6 should be placed where in the passage?
   a. After sentence 1
   b. After sentence 2
   c. After sentence 3
   d. After sentence 4
   e. Left after sentence 5

53. Which edit should be made in sentence 3?
   a. "nor" should be changed to "or"
   b. "seemed" should be changed to "seems"
   c. "me" should be changed to "I"
   d. "attracts" should be changed to "attract"
   e. No edit should be made.

54. How could sentences 6 and 7 best be combined?
    a. Swiftly, I ruled out crawling under as an option and also turning back.
    b. Ruling out two options swiftly: crawling under and turning back.
    c. I swiftly ruled out the options of crawling under or turning back.
    d. I ruled out crawling under as an option and I swiftly also ruled out turning back.
    e. I swiftly ruled out crawling under as an option and also turning back.

55. Which word could be inserted at the beginning of sentence 2 before "confident" to best clarify the meaning?
    a. Even
    b. However
    c. Hardly
    d. Finally
    e. Especially

56. Which of the following is the best way to split sentence 1 into two separate sentences?
    a. I had set out on a journey, with no other purpose than that of exploring a certain province of natural knowledge. I strayed no hair's breadth from the course which it was my right and my duty to pursue; and yet I found that, whatever route I took, before long, I came to a tall and formidable-looking fence.
    b. I had set out on a journey, with no other purpose than that of exploring a certain province of natural knowledge, I strayed no hair's breadth from the course which it was my right and my duty to pursue. Yet I found that, whatever route I took, before long, I came to a tall and formidable-looking fence.
    c. I had set out on a journey, with no other purpose than that of exploring a certain province of natural knowledge, I strayed no hair's breadth from the course which it was my right and my duty to pursue; and yet I found that, whatever route I took, before long. I came to a tall and formidable-looking fence.
    d. I had set out on a journey. With no other purpose than that of exploring a certain province of natural knowledge, I strayed no hair's breadth from the course which it was my right and my duty to pursue; and yet I found that, whatever route I took, before long, I came to a tall and formidable-looking fence.
    e. I had set out on a journey, with no other purpose than that of exploring a certain province of natural knowledge, I strayed no hair's breadth from the course which it was my right and my duty to pursue; and yet. I found that, whatever route I took, before long, I came to a tall and formidable-looking fence.

The following sentences contain either one error or no errors. For questions 57 through 65, select the underlined section that contains the error, or select "E" for "no error."

57. There are some difficulties inherent <u>for moving</u> across the country: <u>one must</u> secure housing <u>remotely</u> and <u>transport</u> belongings great distances.
    a. for moving
    b. one must
    c. remotely
    d. transport
    e. No error

58. <u>When driving</u> on a <u>major</u> road, <u>to have gone</u> the speed limit <u>is prudent</u>.
    a. When driving
    b. major
    c. to have gone
    d. is prudent
    e. No error

59. Salvador <u>and me</u>, <u>who take</u> Spanish class <u>together</u>, often study in the library <u>prior to</u> exams.
    a. and me
    b. who take
    c. together
    d. prior to
    e. No error

60. <u>Because of</u> the stringent law <u>enacted in</u> the state, legislators <u>must be careful</u> to review <u>policies</u>.
    a. Because of
    b. enacted in
    c. must be careful
    d. policies
    e. No error

61. <u>If the candidate</u> the company <u>had endorsed</u> were <u>to win</u>, the CEO <u>is very</u> pleased.
    a. If the candidate
    b. had endorsed
    c. to win
    d. is very
    e. No error

62. Even though we already understood the solution, the tutor insisted on explaining the steps again to Sara and I.
   a. Even though
   b. already understood
   c. insisted on
   d. and I
   e. No error

63. It is essential to applying the criteria uniformly across all of the candidates in order to judge the contest fairly.
   a. applying
   b. criteria
   c. in order to
   d. fairly
   e. No error

64. Leaving home to visit my grandmother, I repeated to myself the three things I had to remember to do: help repair her sink, remind her of the party, and making sure that she had enough heating oil.
   a. to visit
   b. to myself
   c. help repair
   d. making sure
   e. No error

65. Sheila would like to either go to the matinee film nor see the movie tomorrow.
   a. would like
   b. either go
   c. nor see
   d. tomorrow
   e. No error

Writing Section – Answers

Correct answers are given along with a brief explanation of the grammatical or stylistic rule addressed in the question.

1. C – wordiness and precision
2. D – misplaced modifier and wordiness
3. A – parallelism in listing, subject/verb agreement
4. D – word usage
5. A – verb tense
6. D – verb tense
7. C – subject/verb agreement and gerund use
8. E – No error
9. D – imprecise comparisons
10. D – parallelism in listing
11. E – No error
12. B – "one" and "you" cannot both be used as forms of address in the same sentence
13. E – No error
14. A – subject/object pronoun use (Timothy and me)
15. B – subject/verb agreement (difficulty is compounded)
16. D – parallelism (and to contact)
17. B – subject/verb agreement (The way…provides the artist)
18. E – No error
19. C – adjective/adverb use (familiarly although)
20. C – proper idiomatic usage (need for)
21. D – subject/verb agreement (everyone got his or her beverage)
22. C – verb tense (the car will consume)
23. C – subject/object pronoun (David and she went to the store)
24. A – proper idiomatic usage (Regardless of)
25. E – No error
26. B – subject/verb agreement (are comprised)
27. C – pronoun agreement (his or her opinion)
28. C – superlative use (is better, since only two things are being compared)
29. A – adjective/adverb use (menacingly)
30. A – least wordy and most direct
31. D
32. C – Sentence four best sums up the thoughts in sentences 5 and 6.
33. C – Sentence 5 further elaborates the information given in sentence 6
34. D
35. D – A, B, and E are arguably good edits, but D fixes a grammatical mistake
36. C – least wordy option
37. D – verb tense, corrects the sentence fragment
38. A – corrects the sentence fragment
39. B – misplaced modifier

40. D – sentence fragment
41. E – no error
42. A – subject/verb agreement and verb tense
43. C – redundancy
44. D – subject/verb agreement, collective nouns
45. E – no error
46. A – verb tense
47. C – wordiness/verb tense (unnecessary gerund)
48. A – pronoun use
49. B – adjective/adverb use
50. E – no error
51. B
52. D
53. D
54. C
55. B
56. A
57. A – idiomatic usage (inherent in/to moving)
58. C – verb tense (going)
59. A – subject/object pronoun use (and I)
60. E – No error
61. C – verb tense/subjunctive (would be very)
62. D – subject/object pronoun use (and me)
63. A – verb tense (apply)
64. D – parallelism in listing (and make sure)
65. C – word use (or sec)

Chapter 10: Final Thoughts

We wish you the best of luck as you get ready for the PSAT exam. Remember, treat this like you are studying for the "real deal" SAT because it will only help you improve!

If you feel like you did not get the score you wanted on the PSAT and are concerned about preparing for the SAT, we sincerely hope you take note of our advice to seek all the help and guidance you can. There are so many resources out there at your disposal and they are just waiting for you to take advantage of them. Start with your friends. Sometimes, that's all it takes is to lean on a friend and confide you are struggling and they might have advice or a resource you hadn't considered before. Also, it can help to occasionally study with a friend. Just have to have them there as a sounding board for ideas can sometimes help you work through obstacles you are facing in working towards your goal.

If you hit the point where you just aren't making the progress on your own and decide to enlist the help of a tutor, be sure to look around for different options. Now, this doesn't mean any average Joe off the street can help you, but if you are on a budget there are plenty of college students out there who tutor and are very proficient in SAT subjects. Remember, the SAT test is just to get INTO college and the PSAT is just a practice for the SAT (unless you are competing for National Merit Scholar recognition which only about 2% of the country will achieve). It is not testing college level materials. However, there is an obvious importance in finding someone who has experience teaching or tutoring, whether that be a tutoring company or a private tutor. You don't necessarily need to spend thousands of dollars for a good tutor or review course, so use your best judgment for your specific needs.

We wish you the best of luck and happy studying!

Sincerely,

The Accepted, Inc. Team

STUDY SMARTER. SCORE HIGHER. GET ACCEPTED.